EXPLORE
THE GREAT OCEAN ROAD

Geelong to Mt Gambier

Douglas Stone
Greg Dunnett
Derrick Stone

SEE
AUSTRALIA
GUIDES

CONTENTS

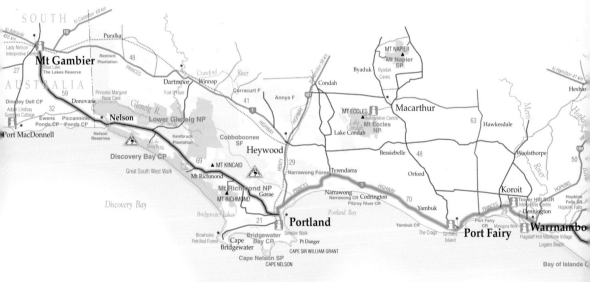

First published 1991
Revised 1997

See Australia Guides Pty Ltd
ACN 005 082 557
'The Valley'
Valley Farm Road
Healesville 3777

ISBN 0 646 06846 6
Copyright
Text: © Douglas Stone, 1997
Cartography: © Greg Dunnett, 1997
Design: © Derrick Stone, 1997

Typeset by See Australia Guides Pty Ltd.

Colour separations by Scanagraphix Pty Ltd, Brunswick, Victoria, Australia.

Printed and bound by Toppan, Hong Kong.

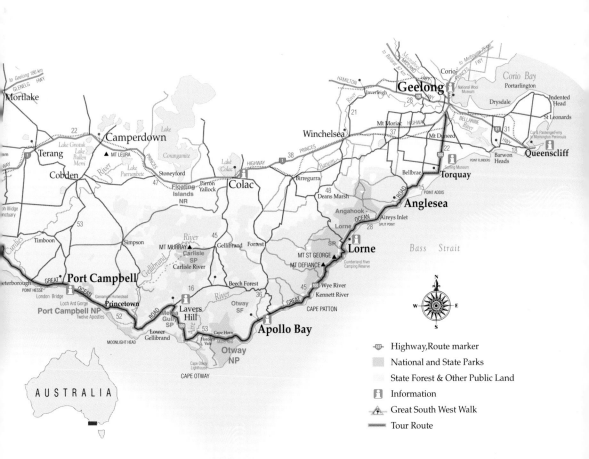

USING THE BOOK

This book leads you through some of Australia's most spectacular coastal country. The 550 kilometre route from Geelong to Mt Gambier twists, climbs, and cuts through towering rainforests with magnificent waterfalls, runs past sheer limestone cliffs, crosses fast flowing streams, and provides a succession of sparkling seascapes.

This guide will help you discover the unique landforms; Aboriginal and European heritage; shipwrecks; hidden waterfalls, secluded beaches and our wonderful flora and fauna in National and State Parks. The route links the capital cities of Melbourne and Adelaide and is a magnificent alternative to the Princes Highway (National Route No.1).

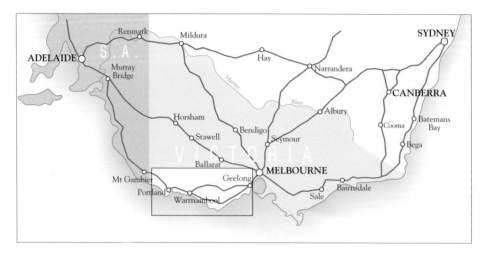

The Maps
The tour route, scenic drives, points of interest, picnic - camping grounds and lookouts are clearly marked. All maps are orientated to north with scale bars included. Road surfaces and intermediate distances between strategic points are indicated.

The Route
The description of the tour route is in declared direction of travel, however all references to points of interest are easily located when travelling in either direction. This guide has been conveniently divided into sections enabling you to plan your trip, maximising your stay at each destination.

KEY TO MAP SYMBOLS USED IN THIS GUIDE

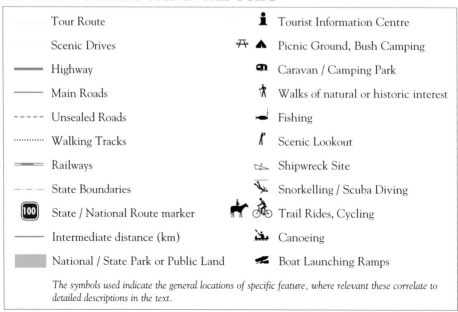

Tour Route	Tourist Information Centre
Scenic Drives	Picnic Ground, Bush Camping
Highway	Caravan / Camping Park
Main Roads	Walks of natural or historic interest
Unsealed Roads	Fishing
Walking Tracks	Scenic Lookout
Railways	Shipwreck Site
State Boundaries	Snorkelling / Scuba Diving
State / National Route marker	Trail Rides, Cycling
Intermediate distance (km)	Canoeing
National / State Park or Public Land	Boat Launching Ramps

The symbols used indicate the general locations of specific feature, where relevant these correlate to detailed descriptions in the text.

• HISTORY AND CONSTRUCTION OF •
THE GREAT OCEAN ROAD

By 1846 much of the coast of the Port Phillip region (Victoria) had been surveyed from the sea. Apart from small areas around the settlements however, the inland was largely undeveloped and inaccessible. Coach roads were eventually formed. But they were rough, sometimes with gradients of 1 in 4, and climbing to heights of 200m then plunging again to sea level. Streams had to be forded, and wide boulder-strewn beaches crossed. Parts of the track could only be passed at low tide during the summer months. Until 1914 little had been done to link these tracks.

In early 1916, Mr W Calder, Chairman of the Country Roads Board proposed to the State War Council that funds should be offered for road construction to employ returned soldiers from World War One. Such a road would be from Barwon Heads to Warrnambool and would be a tourist road 'of world repute, equalling that of California'.

Men with picks, shovels and crow-bars building the Great Ocean Road.

The Great Ocean Road Trust was founded by Hon. Howard Hitchock in 1918, and began work on the first section between Lorne and Cape Patton late in August that year. In September 1919 the second section between Cape Patton and Anglesea was commenced. Massive engineering difficulties had to be overcome, over 3000 ex-servicemen were employed, and they were later joined by the jobless of the Great Depression.

By 1922 the section from Anglesea to Lorne was passable. At first it was just a track cut into the sides of hills and cliffs, where dust, steep gradients, narrow roadways, hairpin bends and treacherous corners had to be negotiated. Returned 'Diggers' named vantage points and various landforms as reminders of World War One, for example the Artillery Rocks, Mt Defiance, Shrapnel Gully and Cinema Point.

Many times it was necessary to repair the road as you negotiated it, this time between Aireys Inlet and Lorne.

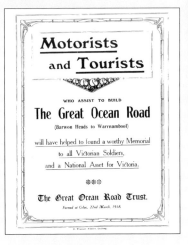

Front cover of the Financial Appeal brochure for the construction of the Great Ocean Road

The first toll gate, at the eastern end, was situated between the Devil's Elbow and Grassy Creek

On 26 November 1932 the Great Ocean Road was officially opened by the Governor Sir William Irvine. Between 1932 and 1936 it was a toll road. The last official act of the Great Ocean Trust was the unveiling of plaques on the Memorial Archway at Ocean View in 1939. The memorial arch stood until 1983, when it was burnt in the Ash Wednesday bush fires on 16 February. The stone supports on each side of the road survived and the arch was rebuilt in 1991.

GEELONG AND THE SURF COAST

GEELONG TO ANGLESEA

National Wool Centre, Geelong

Geelong is Victoria's second largest port.
PREVIOUS PAGES *Marina, Geelong*

Geelong to Anglesea
36 kilometres

Geelong, 72 kilometres from Melbourne, set on the shores of Corio Bay, is Victoria's second largest city. Geelong boasts a wealth of heritage buildings; is liberally provided with parks and gardens plus numerous natural attractions. It is the gateway to the Great Ocean Road, Bellarine Peninsula and the Surf Coast.

Damien Hardman at Jan Juc

The Great Ocean Road was built between 1919 and 1932 as a memorial to the returned service men and women of World War 1 to provide access to some of Australia's most beautiful ocean, mountain and river scenery. Many who did the construction work, with picks and shovels were 'diggers' themselves, in need of work during the Great Depression.

The Great Ocean Road from Aireys Inlet to Warrnambool is one of the great scenic coastal drives of the world. The road is carved into cliffs and mountains bordering Australia's most rugged and densely forested stretch of coastline.

The Bellarine Peninsula, with its rolling hills running to the shores of Port Phillip Bay combines maritime and agricultural heritage and golden beaches. It includes Queenscliff, one of the jewels of Victoria's coastal towns.

The Surf Coast extends from Point Lonsdale to Aireys Inlet and is a continuous chain of spectacular ocean beaches occasionally broken by rocky headlands. Bells Beach just west of Torquay is the most famous, it's consistent, spectacular waves attract the worlds top surfers to compete in the Surf Classic held each Easter. Torquay is the Surf Capital of Australia and a stroll through the 'Surf Coast Plaza' will bring you face to face with local manufactures who dominate the sporting industry both here and overseas.

Geelong

If it wasn't for a sand bar across it's natural harbour Geelong would have been Victoria's capital city. To really appreciate Geelong's beautiful setting a visit to Ceres Lookout is a must. From here you become aware of the pattern of the city parks and gardens as they wrap around the blue waters of Corio Bay. Ceres Lookout is located off the Barrabool Road west of the suburb of Highton.

Shearing shed tapestry, National Wool Museum

AT A GLANCE
GEELONG
Distance:
72 km from Melbourne

Tourist Information:
Geelong Otway Visitors and Convention Bureau
National Wool Museum
Cnr Moorabool and
Brougham Streets,
Geelong Vic. 3220
Phone: (03) 5222 2900

Market Square Tourist/ Community Kiosk
Market Square Shopping Centre
74 Mallop Street,
Geelong Vic. 3220
Phone: (03) 5222 3477

Attractions:
National Wool Museum, Maritime Museum, Art Gallery, Customs House, Botanic Gardens, 'The Heights', 'Barwon Grange', St Albans Homestead, Ceres Lookout, Cunningham Pier, Eastern Beach and Buckley's Falls.

Picnic spots:
Botanic Gardens, Steam Packet Gardens, Balyang Sanctuary, Barwon River Reserve, Buckley's Falls, Eastern Beach and Queens Park.

Geelong was visited by Europeans in 1835, before Melbourne was established. It became the focus of the colony's trade after John Batman reported rich native pastures to the land hungry squatters from Van Diemen's Land (Tasmania). During the 1850s the fertile Western District provided agricultural goods for export and Geelong rose to even greater prominence as the closest port to Victoria's Central Goldfields. Thousands of fortune-seekers disembarked, bought their stores and headed for the Ballarat diggings. 1857 saw the linking of Melbourne and Geelong by rail.

Manufacturing has played a major role in the city's development. In 1852 Donaghy's rope-making factory (thought to be the first in Australia) was opened and in 1856 James Harrison of Geelong developed the world's first commercial refrigeration system in the town. The advent of Geelong's large petrochemical and car manufacturing industries in the 1920s created one of Australia's busiest and most accessible waterfronts.

Geelong Waterfront
The whole of Geelong's city waterfront is undergoing a period of rejuvenation. In 1993 the art deco Eastern Beach Swimming Enclosure was re-opened having been restored to its former glory. This development continues, with the new Woolstores campus of Deakin University retaining the facade of the Dalgety Woolstores on the waterfront. Restaurants overlook the bay and the marina. At the eastern end of the foreshore an avenue of huge palms leads to the Eastern Beach Swimming enclosure.

Packington Street is a favourite hangout for locals and visitors 'in the know', who come to meet friends in the many coffee shops, or to do some specialty shopping. This tree-lined street features clusters of antique shops, specialty decorating, clothing, and homewares shops, to cake shops and coffee houses which are local institutions. Many of the original 19th century shop fronts remain.

The northern end is the most lively, with many restaurants, a huge range of shopping and the historic Geelong West Town Hall. Opposite the town hall is the old blue-stone Uniting Church of St Phillips, originally built as a Methodist church in 1868.

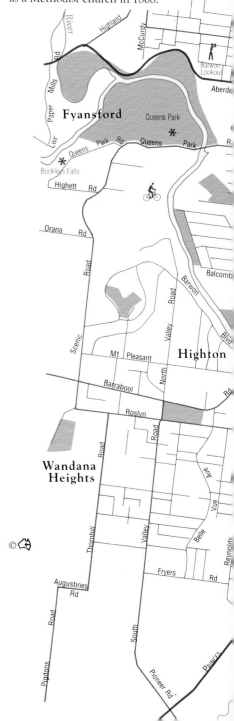

In the fine Botanic Gardens, Eastern Park, you can see the first Customs House (relocated several times), a prefabricated timber building which was later used as a telegraph station.

An excellent 'Heritage Trail' map has been produced by the Geelong Historical Society and is available at the Tourist Information Centre for a small charge. Another way to discover Geelong is via the numerous bicycle tracks which run along the foreshore and criss-cross the city and suburbs.

A great way to explore Geelong's water front is to leave the car at Rippleside Park and cycle or walk along the Bob McGovan Path which runs through the foreshore reserve to Cunningham Pier and Steampacket Gardens. From the water front follow Moorabool Street, to the National Wool Centre and the heart of the City.

Leaving the freeway

When approaching Geelong from Melbourne turn off the Princes Highway at Bell Parade. Rippleside Park is on your left and is an excellent place to break the journey with childrens play equipment, picnic and barbecue facilities set on lawns running to the water's edge. Turn right into the Esplanade

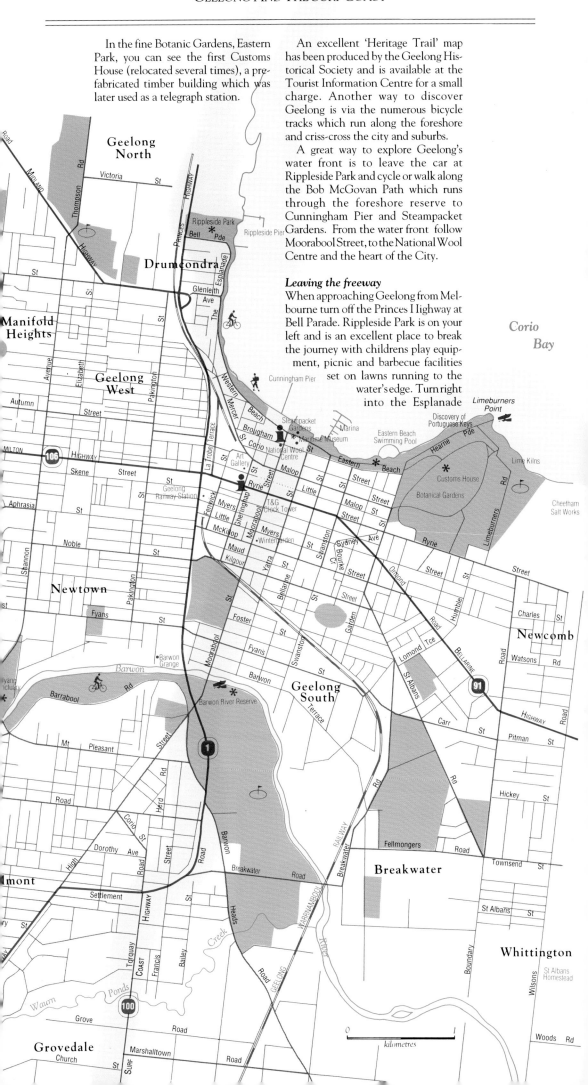

Examining the clip, National Wool Museum

Shearing shed interior at the Wool Museum

NATIONAL WOOL MUSEUM

Interior of the Geelong Art Gallery displaying *A Bush Burial*, 1890 oil on canvas, 122.5 x 224.5cm by Frederick McCubbin. It was prevoiusly thought that the site of the painting was in the bush at Blackburn, but now a second location of 'artists camp' at Box Hill has been suggested. No matter where the painting was sited, it was hailed in 1890 as 'a pure product of Australia.'

which skirts Port Phillip Bay and veer left into Western Beach which follows the water front to the City Centre. There is ample parking here to leave the vehicle or bike and stroll through the network of gardens, piers and marinas. Downtown Geelong and the Tourist Information Centre situated at The National Wool Museum are only half a block away at the corner of Moorabool and Brougham Streets.

Major Attractions

The National Wool Museum is housed in the Dennys Lascelles' bluestone woolstore built in 1872 at the bay end of Moorabool Street.

The showpiece of the centre is an exhibition of Australia's wool industry, past, present and future. The smells, feel and folklore surrounding wool since McArthur's introduction of the first sheep in the 1800s is brought to life.

The display spreads over three galleries. *Gallery One* focuses on the human effort involved producing sheep and wool. *Gallery Two* depicts wool processing and the textile industry. *Gallery Three* exhibits bales of wool, sample boxes and an animated model.

The all important wool auctions are still conducted here throughout the year and visitors are welcome to sit in and see Western District graziers and international buyers in action. The National Wool Museum also includes

shopping arcades with a selection of Australian hand-knitted pullovers and woollen garments, Australian traditional stockmen clothing, antiques, Australiana and works of art.

Open: Daily 10am–5pm. Closed Christmas Day and Good Friday. Admission is charged to the Museum.

Geelong Art Gallery, Little Malop Street was established in 1896, following a meeting chaired by banker and amateur artist, J.W.Sayer, a member of the Geelong Progress League. In 1913 land was allocated by the City of Geelong and the construction of the new building was funded largely through public subscription.

The Collection The Geelong community established a tradition of supporting its Gallery in 1900 when a public subscription purchased Frederick McCubbin's work *A Bush Burial*. This first work is still recognised as one of the galleries best. Works by other 19th Century artists include Eugene von Guerard, Louis Buvelot, Tom Roberts, Arthur Streeton, and Walter Withers. They contrast with the more modern works of Fred Williams, John Firth-Smith, and Peter Booth. There is a complete set of Eric Thake Christmas cards, and colonial watercolours depicting the Geelong region.

Guided tours are conducted each Wednesday at 2.30pm followed by afternoon tea. Group tours can be arranged by contacting the Gallery on (03) 5229 3645.

Open: Tuesday–Friday, 10am–5pm, weekends 1pm–5pm. Admission is charged.

Wintergarden 51 McKillop Street, was a former church, built in 1854. The classic building has been transformed into a refined venue for speciality shops, including a restaurant, antique dealer, individually designed clothing, elegant knitwear, giftware and other treasures.

Open: Daily 9.30am–6pm.

Along the Waterfront

Port of Geelong Authority's - Maritime Museum, 65 Brougham St. The centrepiece of the museum is a section of the original wharf, with bollards, ropes, cargo and the early equipment used to load sailing ships during the 18th Century. Displays depict Aboriginal culture, early European exploration and settlement, shipping disasters, navigation, agriculture, industrial development and the steam era.
Open: Wednesday 9am–12noon, Sat 2pm–5pm. Admission is free.

H. M. Customs House Brougham Place, across the intersection from the National Wool Centre was designed by the Colonial Architect James Balmain and built in 1855-56 by W G Cornish for the the Public Works Office. The basic structure is basalt rubble, clad in Barrabool sandstone ashlar and is one of the finest mid-19th Century public buildings in western Victoria. It will remind you of the old Hobart Town architecture. It is one of the oldest Government Buildings in Australia still serving it's original function.

Since 1856 H.M.Customs House has serviced the trade and commerce of Geelong and district by collecting tariffs, controlling the entry of prohibited imports and preventing the export of native birds and animals.

Cunningham Pier is a wide concrete structure with storage sheds, cranes and a central railway line. Tug boats and large merchant ships often berth here. The pier is open to the public during daylight hours and is a popular local fishing spot. It's construction started in October 1854. It was extended to its present length of 305m and 4.5m depth in 1861.

Next to Cunningham Pier are the **Steampacket Gardens** where basalt retainer walls are broken by small jetties jutting into the bay. Benches in the paved areas interspersed through the landscaped gardens offer a great place to sit and soak up Geelong's waterfront atmosphere, especially on a hot summer's evening. A statue of Albert Edward Prince of Wales, later King Edward the VII overlooks the scene.

Royal Geelong Yacht Club and Marina

Rows of yachts are literally stacked on the pavement of Eastern Beach, demonstrating the locals passion for sailing. The club was founded in March 1859 with 35 members. The club obtained it's Royal Charter in 1924.

Eastern Beach, now restored, is classified by the National Trust. It is very popular with locals, and in summer, families flock to catch the cooler breezes coming off the bay while children swim safely. There is a kiosk

The Maritime Museum

popular with families, the bistro is fully licensed and offers al fresco dining (and live music on the weekends). Upstairs the restaurant offers stunning views across the bay to the You Yangs. Eastern Beach joins the Geelong Botanical Gardens. There are excellent picnic facilities with electric barbeques, picnic shelters, swimming enclosure with slide, childrens' pool and fountains. The adventure playground is well equipped and bollards stand amongst the picnickers. No: alcohol, camping, ball games. Dogs, bikes and boards only on designated paths.

Lime Kilns are located at the end of Limeburners Road on the eastern boundary of the Geelong Gun Club, East Geelong. These three brick and stone kilns are among the oldest lime kilns in Victoria and are important industrial archaeological sites. Built c. 1852 into the cliff-face, they remain virtually intact although partly buried.

The Rotary Club of Geelong has erected a monument overlooking the low cliffs at Limeburners Point to record the finding of the **Portuguese Keys** in 1847. The find has been a mystery ever since the keys were unearthed 4m below the surface of Limeburner Bourchier's kiln and reported by Governor La Trobe. The keys are thought to have belonged to a Portuguese expedition lead by Cristovao De Mendonca which visited the coast in 1522. The keys have since been lost.

Eastern Beach swimming enclosure

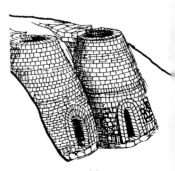
Artists impression of the once active kilns. Such kilns were sited on the side of a hill to aid draught and top loading of the fuel and chunks of limestone. After three days' burning at about 1000°C, the kiln was allowed to cool, ready for drawing off the lime. The whole cycle took about 6 days.

The remains of the lime kilns

Transport Services:
There are frequent rail services between Melbourne and Geelong daily. Rail links continue to Colac, Camperdown, Terang, Warrnambool, and Ballarat.

Luxury road coaches, operate daily to Anglesea, Aireys Inlet, Lorne and Apollo Bay along the Great Ocean Road. This service is extended to Port Campbell, Peterborough and Warrnambool every Friday. During the peak tourist season in December and January the service through to Warrnambool is available on Mondays and Fridays.

For information
Phone: 132 232

Accommodation:
25 Motels
5 Hotels
9 Caravan Parks

Fishing:
Eastern Beach Boat Hire,
42 Apex Ave, Belmont (03) 5243 4306 for half cabin cruisers and run-abouts for fishing in Corio and Port Phillip Bays. Boat launching ramp at Limeburners Point.
Jetties: Snapper have been caught at night. Black Trevally mass around the wharfs during February.
Corio Bay: Snapper, Flathead and sharks are caught in the bay as well as the outer channels.

Johnstone Park

On the tip of Limeburners Point is a boat launching ramp, jetties, an extensive car-park and toilets. It is a favourite fishing spot, with views across to Point Henry, east to the city of Geelong and to the You Yang Ranges.

Conservatory, Botanic Gardens

Parks and Gardens
Geelong Botanic Gardens are located in Eastern Park. Botanist Daniel Bunce, Director of the Geelong Botanic Gardens began planting in 1858 and transformed a large unfenced wilderness into the nucleus of the splendid gardens seen today. The gardens are landscaped around the highest point of Eastern Park and command spectacular views of Corio Bay. The plantings include an extensive range of Australian flora with many rare and endangered species. A large conservatory with tropical and seasonal displays of geraniums is another feature.

The **Old Customs House,** reputed to be the oldest wooden building in Victoria, reputedly prefabricated in Sydney in 1838, has been resited in the gardens. It was Geelong's first telegraph station and relayed the first dramatic news of the Eureka Stockade Rebellion in 1852 to the government in Melbourne. Historic photographs and relics are displayed inside.
Open: Daily 9am–5pm.

Guided tours of the Botanic Gardens leave from the front gates every Wednesday at 10.30am. From October to March they are also conducted on Sundays at 2.30pm. Group tours can be arranged by phoning the Director, Geelong Botanic Gardens on (03) 5227 0386. The tour takes approximately 1.5 hours and is free.

Next to the Botanic Gardens in Eastern Park are large picnic shelters with electric barbecues.

Johnstone Park This park, bounded by Gheringhap, Fenwick and Malop Streets, began its history as LaTrobe Dam, supplying water for sheep. It soon became a local dumping ground for rubbish, but in 1867 civic minded citizens began its conversion to a park. In 1872 it was officially opened and named after the mayor of Geelong, Robert de Bruce Johnstone.

The grassed banks of the old dam enclose a central colonial bandstand with paths radiating out through tall palms. The old world atmosphere is enhanced by the Art Gallery and War Memorial which overlook the park. On Christmas Day 1852 bushranger Captain Melville (Frank McCallum) was captured near the dam, no doubt while watering his horses. A plaque located at the entrance of the park on Gheringhap Street commemorates the capture .

Important Civic Buildings
An **Historic Mural** is housed in the State Government Offices, cnr Lt Malop Street and Fenwick Street. The history of the Geelong region, its agriculture, industry, sport, transport and people, is depicted in this 30m long mosaic mural.

Old Telegraph Station Ryrie Street. This building of Barrabool sandstone was erected in 1857, to become the town's third telegraph station. In 1870 it became the postmaster's residence. For many years a black time ball on a pole on the tower roof dropped daily at 1pm, enabling mariners at the waterfront to adjust their chronometers. The building has since been used by various government departments, and is now classified by the National Trust.

Post Office Ryrie Street. In 1891, Geelong's postal services were improved with the construction of this post office building. In 1912 the first automatic telephone exchange in Australia was opened in Geelong. Three years later the clock and bell mechanisms were installed as a memorial to Edward VII.

Town Hall cnr Gheringhap and Lt Malop Streets. The building of this two-storey Classical building was started in 1855 and completed in 1917. It is one of the oldest halls in Victoria still in use.

T&G Clock Tower cnr Moorabool and Ryrie Streets. This unusual clock has two life size bronze figures, the Farmer and his Son, in working garb who emerge to strike each hour. It symbolises the father handing over to his son and urging him to carry on the good work. It echoes Geelong's close ties with it's rural heritage.

Churches on the Hill
The hill bounded by Maude, Moorabool and Yarra Streets is literally dotted with spires. Stroll through the grounds and inspect the interiors of these fine old churches. The views of Corio Bay and the You Yangs, the steep granitic hills to the east are outstanding from this part of the city.

Christ Church 57 Moorabool Street, is Victoria's oldest Anglican church still in use. The foundation stone was laid in 1843 by Bishop Broughton. It was finally built between 1845 and 1847 from drawings by the Bishop's Sydney architects. Extensions were completed in 1855, and interior alternations made in 1870, 1920 and 1962. The tower has been rendered to protect the deteriorating Ceres stone.

St Mary of the Angels Cathedral cnr Yarra and Myers Street. This fine Gothic Cathedral can be seen from most parts of Geelong and the surrounding district.

Father Stephens conducted the first service in a small weatherboard chapel on this site in 1842. The chapel was replaced by a larger stone church in 1846. However because of the prosperity generated by Victoria's gold rushes it was decided in 1854 that this prime site overlooking the city warranted the construction of a stately cathedral. The church was consecrated in 1872, but the spires, transepts, sanctuary and tower were not added until the 1930s.

Wesley Church 96 Yarra Street. In 1846 a permanent Methodist church was built on this site at a cost of nearly £500. The only portion of the old church still standing is the south side. In 1854 a transept was added. In 1858 the church was widened and in 1932 a narthex and chapel were added.

St Johns Lutheran Church 165 Yarra Street was Geelong's first Presbyterian church, built in 1841-42. The stuccoed Classical front was added in 1912, when it became the home of the Communna-Feinne Society.

St Johns' is believed to be Geelong's oldest masonry building.

St George's Presbyterian Church cnr Ryrie Street and LaTrobe Terrace, is a Gothic Revival church designed by Nathaniel Billing and built c. 1861. The transepts, vestibule, spire and tower were later additions. Other examples of Billing's work are at Port Fairy.

Synagogue The Jewish population requested land as a burial ground in the 1840s, but it was not until 1854 that the first synagogue was built in Yarra Street. By 1861 the gold rush had increased the Jewish population sufficiently for the larger synagogue to be erected.

Former Geelong Grammar School 55 Maude Street, was built in 1857 to a prize-winning Backhouse and Reynolds design. The south wing of this Gothic Revival building of cement rendered basalt, was occupied by Geelong Grammar School until 1914. Now it is the Reformed Theological College.

Grand houses
'Corio Villa' 56 Eastern Beach. The original section of this building, an imported iron house made by a Glasgow

'Corio Villa'

iron-foundry, was assembled in 1856. Extensions were made in 1890. The original owner died in 1854, before the building materials arrived in Geelong in 1855. The cumbersome materials remained unclaimed, and were sold to Alfred Douglass at a bargain price by the port authorities. No assembly plans could be found and Douglass wrote to Scotland for the plans but found they had been burnt with the foundry. So the house was assembled piece by piece like a jigsaw. The walls of the original prefabricated portion consist of cast-iron plate fitted and bolted together, with cast-iron sash windows. The building rests on bluestone foundations.

'The Heights' 140 Aphrasia Street, Newtown, was prefabricated in Germany and built for Charles Ibbotson in 1855. The fourteen roomed timber mansion is the largest of all German houses erected in Victoria. The mansion is set in beautiful gardens with a wide sweeping driveway. It has an unusual stone water tower and extensive outbuildings.

'The Heights' underwent extensive renovations in 1939, but still retains the character of a complete 1850s estate.
Open: Saturday, Sun and Public Holidays, 2pm–5pm and by appointment. Closed Christmas Day and Good Friday. Admission is charged.

'Barwon Grange', Fernleigh Street, Newtown. This Gothic style house set in beautiful gardens overlooking the Barwon River was built in 1856 for J.P. O'Brien, a local merchant-ship builder. It is now managed by the National Trust.

'Barwon Grange' a National Trust property

St Mary of the Angels Cathedral

NORTH SHORE INDUSTRIAL DRIVE
Leaving Geelong on the Princes Highway heading towards Melbourne, take the underpass onto Corio Quay Road and the suburb of Geelong North. Pass the massive wheat silos and the **Bulk Wheat Wharf**. Turn right into The Esplanade and see the **Ford Motor Company of Australia**, **Lascelles Wharf** with its berths 1 and 2 and the container berth. Turn left into Maddens Avenue and then right into Seabeach Parade, which has three name changes in quick succession from Lowe Street to Wharf Road and then to Shell Parade. To your right is the **Shell Co. of Australia**, **Wharf Refinery Pier** and on your left are the massive works of the **Shell Oil Refinery**. Turning right into Foreshore Road you travel from the industrial heartland to the academic and traditional world of **Geelong Grammar School** where the foundation stone was laid on 3 April 1913. **Limeburners Bay** is on your right. Retrace your drive and turn right into Shell Parade and follow it through to the Princes Highway, or turn left at School Road, pass over the Melbourne–Geelong railway, turn left into Princes Highway and return to Geelong.

Buckley's Falls

William Buckley, an
exceptional man

Barwon Grange is brick with a slate roof, attic rooms and a detached kitchen. The house has an exceptionally picturesque roof line with fretted bargeboards and wooden finials. The verandah design is also unusual, incorporating coupled posts and a decorative balustrade above the roofline. The house is elegantly furnished with period pieces. *Open:* Saturday, Sun and Public Holidays, 2pm–5pm. Closed Christmas Day and Good Friday. Admission is charged.

St Albans Homestead, Homestead Drive, Whittington. The stately 33 roomed homestead, established since 1871 is one of Geelongs most gracious homes and has had a long and colourful history in the racing world. For many years the stud bred horses destined for the race track, and gained fame in 1930 as the place where Phar Lap was hidden before the Melbourne Cup. Visitors can still see Phar Lap's stables and are welcome to tour the homestead. *Open:* Daily- Meals and backpacker accomodation available.

Balyang Sanctuary Lower Shannon Avenue, Newtown, is a small lake where you can view and feed native and introduced water-birds in a natural environment.

Barwon Riverside Reserve, Belmont, provides excellent rowing and boating facilities including a boat ramp, picnic tables and large expanses of lawn. The Head-of-the-river college rowing races are conducted here each April. Bicycle tracks follow the river banks upstream to Queens Park and down stream around the Barwon Valley Golf Club.

Buckley's Falls off Scenic Road, Newtown, are named after William Buckley the escaped convict who lived with the local Aboriginal tribes for 32 years. A walking track runs from the picnic area to the picturesque waterfalls and rapids. White water canoeists negotiate a slalom course through the rapids here. From the lookout in the park you can see the water-powered paper mill on the opposite bank.

• WILLIAM BUCKLEY—THE WILD WHITEMAN •

'You've got two chances—Buckley's, and none'

Sullivans Bay near Sorrento was the first European settlement attempted in Victoria. In 1803 the colonising party was formed in England under the charge of Lieutenant David Collins. It included 51 marines, 12 administrators, 17 free settlers, a missionary and his wife, and 307 convicts.

William Buckley then 20 years old was convicted in Sussex on 2 August 1802 for 'criminally receiving' and sentenced to transportation for life. He escaped from the Victorian settlement with five others on the night of 27 December 1803. They were challenged by guards and one convict was shot. Buckley and his four remaining companions made their way around Port Phillip and attempted to live off the land.

They became so despondent when reaching Swan Island that they lit fires and hung their clothing in trees trying to attract the attention of the ships moored a short distance away across the water, in Sullivans Bay. The dread of punishment was great, but the prospect of starving in the wilderness was even more horrific, but the rescue never came.

William Buckley struck out alone, determined not to give himself up, while his four companions began the trek back around the bay to the safety of the settlement and surrender of their freedom.

After abandoning the settlement, Lt. Collins recorded in Tasmania on 28 July 1805 that Buckley and his companions had 'perished miserably in the woods'.

However, Buckley managed to survive on shell fish off rocks around the coast. He made a makeshift shelter on the rocky slopes of Mt Defiance which had stopped his westward progress along the coast. He was found by local Aboriginal tribesmen who fed and sheltered him until he regained his strength. The Aborigines presumed Buckley was a recarnated chief and called him *Murrangurk* and so he was accepted into the tribe. He spent 32 years, hunting, fighting and learning their languages. He travelled northwest to the lakes on the basalt plains surrounding Lake Corangamite and into the catchments of the Barwon and Moorabool Rivers.

When Buckley finally made contact with a new wave of white settlers at Indented Head on 6 July 1835, he was described as a majestic figure measuring six feet seven inches tall, bronzed by exposure to the weather with flowing hair and beard, cloaked in a kangaroo rug and bearing native weapons.

William Buckley gained a free pardon from Governor Arthur on 28 August 1835 and acted as a guide and interpreter for John Batman and other pioneers in opening up the Port Phillip district.

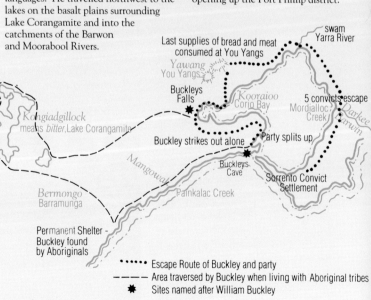

Last supplies of bread and meat
consumed at You Yangs

swam
Yarra River

Yawang
You Yangs

Buckleys
Falls

Kooraioo
Corio Bay

5 convicts escape

Mordialloc
Creek

Kongiadgillock
means *bitter*, Lake Corangamite

Buckley strikes out alone

Party splits up

Mangowak

Buckleys
Cave

Sorrento Convict
Settlement

Bermongo
Barramunga

Painkalac Creek

Permanent Shelter -
Buckley found
by Aboriginals

•••••• Escape Route of Buckley and party
– – – Area traversed by Buckley when living with Aboriginal tribes
✱ Sites named after William Buckley

The Surf Coast

The Surf Coast is a continuous chain of spectacular ocean beaches stretching from Point Lonsdale to Aireys Inlet. The Princes Highway (Hwy No1) takes you through Geelong, crosses the Barwon River and onto the Surf Coast Highway (Route 100) to Torquay.

AT A GLANCE
TORQUAY
Distance:
95km from Melbourne

Information:
Surfworld Australia
Surf Coast Plaza
Beach Road West
Torquay 3228
Phone: (03) 5261 4606

Surfing

In the 1770s Captain Cook recorded surfing in the Hawaiian Islands. Surfing was probably introduced to Australia in 1915 by the Hawaiian, Duke Kahanamoku (the human fish), a quietly spoken Olympic swimming champion. It has since grown into a national passion as more and more people take to the waves. The quality of the Surf Coast waves attracts Australian and overseas champions.

TORQUAY

The towns economy revolves around the surf. Torquay, Jan Juc and Bells Beaches are internationally renowned. Each Easter international and national contestants flock to the Surf Classic at Bells Beach where they come to compete in and enjoy the carnival atmosphere.

The world's largest surfing museum is located in the Surf Coast Plaza. 'Surfworld' is an interactive museum and exhibition celebrating the excitement, history and achievements of Australian surfing.

Open: Daily, admission charged.

Shops in the Plaza are linked by board walkways, capturing the coastal atmosphere. It comes to life during the summer months with young and old

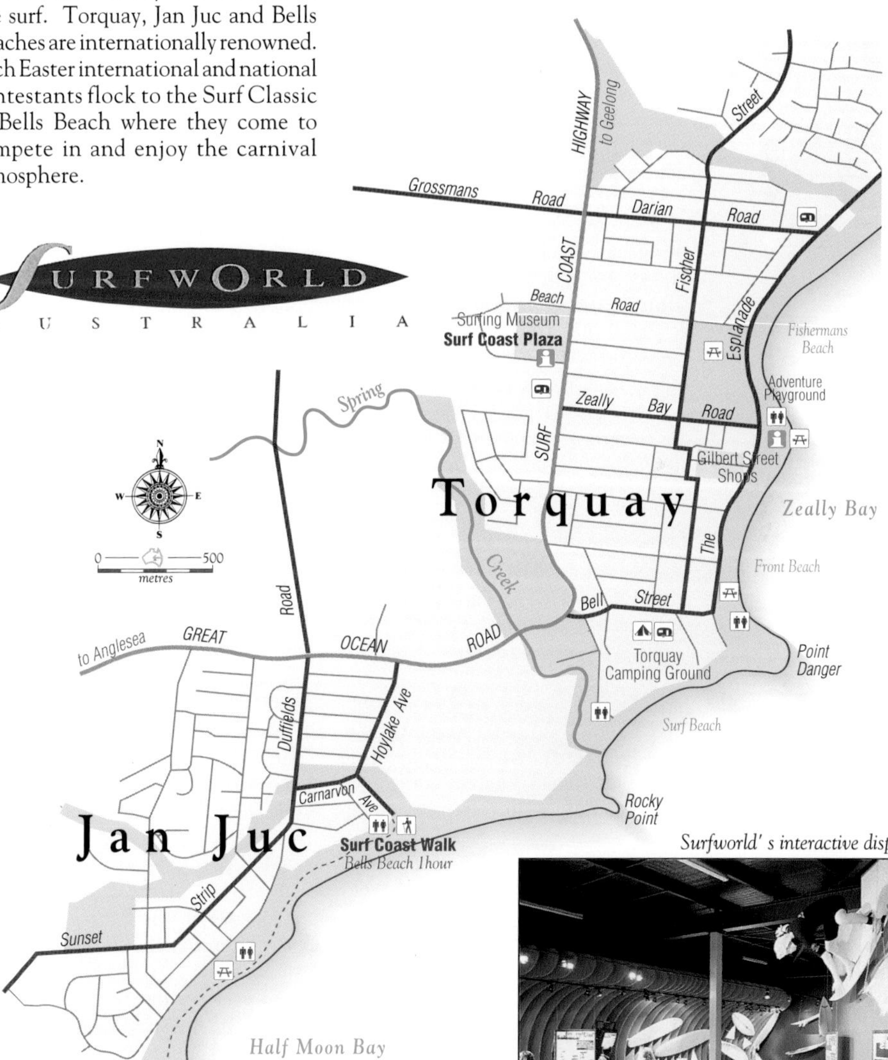

Surfworld's interactive displays

Jason Ribinik at Lorne Point

Early 'Malibu' rider at Bells Beach

TORQUAY

Attractions:
Surf beaches, Bushwalks,
Surf Coast Walk,
Windsurfing at
Pt Danger.

Picnic areas:
Taylor Park

Accommodation:
5 Motels
5 Caravan Parks
10 Bed & Breakfast

Bird watching:
POINT ADDIS
Range of seabirds such as
albatross, gulls, petrels
and prions. Bush birds
such as Rufous Bristlebird
and the Southern Emu-
wren are present, as are
occasional sightings of
the Peregrine Falcon.
Also the site is a roosting
area for the Bent-wing
bat.

congregating to see and buy the latest surfing gear. A browse through the plaza is a must, with surf shops carrying boards, wetsuits, swim wear and every conceivable surfing accessory. The brand names that dominate the surfing industry both here and overseas are Rip Curl, Piping Hot, Watercooled and Quick Silver, companies that developed in Torquay either building surf boards or making surf gear.

The sun, the sand and the water are a perfect combination here for surfing, swimming, sailing, diving and fishing. There is a boat-launching ramp at Fishermen's Beach where the Torquay Sailing Club operates alongside a small fishing fleet.

The front beach is a scenic picnic location too. Majestic Norfolk Island pines shade the sloping lawns bordering the beach. A monument commemorating the first Bass Strait crossing by air by Arthur Long in 1919 is found in a garden bed overlooking the beach.

The back beach is a complete contrast. Bounded by rugged cliffs, it takes the force of the Southern Ocean and produces some great surf. You'll get fine views from the car-park on top of the cliffs.

There are also the historic Bellbrae Carriages and the **Bellbrae Health Resort**, craft shops and galleries, many fine restaurants and modern shopping facilities to visit.

Jan Juc

Neighbouring Jan Juc is another popular swimming and surfing beach. It is separated from Torquay by the golf course which runs from the Great Ocean Road to the coastal dunes. The Jan Juc Surf Life Saving Club and a new four tiered car park and viewing platforms are located off Carnarvon Avenue. From the viewing vantage points you have an uninterrupted view from the cliff top to the surfers below.

The **Surf Coast Walk** starts at Jan Juc and heads along the coast to Aireys Inlet. The entire walk takes approximately 12 hours, however it can be broken into a series of short walks (refer to page 19).

As you leave Jan Juc the Rose Gardens Nursery and Tearooms are on your right.

Bells Beach

Bells Beach is one of the best surfing beaches in the world. Surfing die-hards can be seen here in their wetsuits, even in the chilly depths of winter.

Named after the Bell family who owned land in the area last century, the beaches surfing potential was discovered by Vic Tantau and Owen Yateman in 1949. Early enthusiasts had to lug their gear through trackless scrub and down to the sea or alternately paddle around from Torquay.

Bells became the site for the World Surfing Championships in 1970 and was later proclaimed by an Act of Parliament a 'Surfing Recreation Reserve'.

On a good day, distinct swell lines can be seen moving shoreward in sets of four or more, forming the classic Bells hollow 3 to 4 metre wave. With no headlands enclosing it, Bells Beach is swept by huge swells. The combine forces of spring tides and a strong northwesterly wind create a huge surf up to 6 metres (1981 Championships).

Point Addis The lookout on the point takes in magnificent coastal scenery. A walkway leads west from the car-park, down to an excellent surf beach. Toilet and picnic facilities are located in the tea-tree a short distance back from the point.

The Point Addis Road borders the **Iron Bark Basin** which is a unique tract of bush in near to its natural state stretching east back to Bells Beach. The basin was purchased by the Victorian Government in 1972 from Miss A.K Bell and set aside as a wildlife and fauna reserve.

A car-park and information board are located on the Point Addis Road about 500m from the Great Ocean Road intersection. A network of walking tracks begins at the car-park so you can explore the forest, coastal heathlands, abandoned jarosite mine and secluded beaches. Remember to take binoculars as the bird life is prolific and ranges from blue wrens to peregrine falcons. The Surf Coast Walk passes through the Basin from Bells Beach to Point Addis (refer to Surf Coast Walk- track notes page 19).

SURF COAST WALK
Jan Juc to Bells Beach Walk
Distance: 3km *Time:* 1 hr *Grade:* easy
The walk starts at the Jan Juc Apex Park. Follow the Jan Juc sign from the Great Ocean Road, along Duffields Road then turn left into Carnarvon Avenue.

From the western end of the car-park the track follows the cliff tops providing beautiful views of the beach below. Follow it along a fence line for 1km to a small car-park at the southern fringe of Jan Juc, from here the path continues as a rough 4WD track running southwards through coastal heath. Eventually a white marker, the entrance to Bells Beach, will be visible. Descend through the small gully then climb the hill to the road near the marker. Follow it a short distance to Bells Beach and its access walkways to the surf below.

Bells Beach to Point Addis Walk
Distance: 5km *Time:* 1.75 hrs *Grade:* easy
From the Great Ocean Road take either Bells Boulevard or Jarosite Road to the car-park overlooking the surf beach.

Follow the access track to the beach and continue west across a gully then climb steps to a well-defined track. This continues through tea-tree to the South Side car-park. From here the track follows the road to the top of the hill where a marked walking track heads off across the heathland to the south. Follow this around the head of a small gully to reach a 4WD road. The walking track crosses this road and drops down to a breached dam and the ruins of a jarosite mine. The mine operated until 1927 and supplied deep red ochre to tint paint used on Melbourne's suburban train network in the 1920s. The pigment was so striking that the trains became known affectionately as the 'red rattlers'.

Explore the mine which covered over 100 hectares and includes old buildings and a tramline leading to the beach. Forest regrowth has reclaimed most of the area.

The marked trail climbs inland around the northern rim of Iron Bark Basin. You will catch some fine views through the trees down into the basin and the sea beyond. The marked trail leaves the car-park near the information board and plunges down into the basin. The walk takes you through pleasant iron bark forest, until closer to the cliffs, the trees become more stunted and give way to coastal heathland. The track then climbs to the south up a hill, where Point Addis and Jarosite Headland are clearly visible. Continue until another walking track is intersected running parallel to the bitumen road leading down to Point Addis. This track descends until it meets a beach-access

Grass-tree and natural bush land near Point Addis

SURF COAST WALK

Austral Grass-tree (Xanthorrhoea australis). It is a very large perennial herb, which develops a trunk with age, and supports a dense crown of bluish-green grass-like leaves. The flower heads can grow up to 3m tall.

*Early morning dew on a
Heathland walk*

AT A GLANCE
ANGLESEA
Distance:
108 km from Melbourne

Attractions:
Kangaroos on Anglesea
Golf Course, Trail
Riding, Coogoorah Park,
Point Roadknight, and
Anglesea River foreshore.

Accommodation:
4 Caravan Parks
3 Motels

*Morning mist clings to
Anglesea Inlet*

track which can be followed up to the
road. Turn south-east down the road
and follow it to the car-park at Point
Addis. Toilets and an information board
are situated nearby.

Point Addis to Anglesea Walk
Distance: 7km *Time:* 2 hours *Grade:* easy
From the Point Addis car-park take the
fenced access track to the beach and
follow it for 1.5km to the mouth of a
small creek, next to a rocky headland
(Black Rock). The track leaves the beach
via the creek entrance and climbs inland into cleared land where a vehicle
track starts. As the road climbs around
the cliff tops, it enters bushland and
passes into Eumeralla Scout Camp.

There are some spectacular views in
both directions along the coast from
vantage points along the cliffs. Just
before the first buildings of the camp,
when the road begins to swing west,
pick up the walking track along the cliff
tops and follow it as it descends to the
coastal heathlands below. Continue
along the track as it proceeds towards
Anglesea which you will see ahead.
Take the road closest to the beach around
to the mouth of the Anglesea River.
Walk upstream to the Great Ocean
Road bridge and cross into the parkland
bordering the river where there are
picnic facilities and toilets

Anglesea to Aireys Inlet Walk
Distance: 10 km *Time:* 3 hours
Grade: medium difficulty
At Anglesea the Surf Coast Walk leaves
the beaches and swings inland past the
golf course, famous for the kangaroos
grazing the fairways. Follow a ridge
overlooking the Great Ocean Road to
Aireys Inlet. This walk is particularly
beautiful during spring when the
wildflowers are in bloom.

Cross the Great Ocean Road to enter
Noble Street and immediately turn right
into River Reserve Road. After you
enter Coogoorah Park, follow the foot
path on the eastern side of the road
along the river, crossing the swampy
areas on broadwalks and bridges. Take
time to watch the water birds here.

Soon you reach a gravel road, where
you turn left (west) for 100m to reach a
road junction. Turn south on this road

and soon the marked trail can be picked
up following a walking track on the
right side of the road. The foot track
wanders through the bush, soon becoming a 4WD track following power
lines. It becomes again a walking track
which meanders above the golf course
and past the kangaroos. The track leads
to a sealed road which takes you to Mt
Ingoldsby. The last section is a steep
climb to the top where you are rewarded
with fine views of Anglesea. The road
now meets a main gravel road . Head
south-west (right). After .75km the
trail picks up a 4WD track crossing the
heathland, and here there are spectacular views of the coast in both
directions. There is a steep descent into
Hutt Gully and an equally steep climb
up a hill where the track becomes a
sealed road (Gilbert Street) leading to a
junction with Boundary Road.

Here you have several choices. One
is to turn left into Boundary Road,
which crosses the Great Ocean Road on
the northern limits of Aireys Inlet, which
takes you into town. Another option is
to continue walking along Boundary
Road to the coast where you pick up
the Cliff Walk, a meandering track
which leads to the lighthouse or you can
turn right and follow Boundary Road
west to Bambra Road where a right turn
leads to Distillery Creek Picnic Area.

ANGLESEA
As you sweep down through timbered
cuttings into the township of Anglesea
you will pass a large open cut coal mine
with columns of steam rising to the
north. This is the site of **Alcoa of Australia**, the Anglesea open-cut brown
coal mine and power station. The 150-
megawatt station generates 45% of the
energy needs of the company's aluminium smelter at Point Henry,
Geelong. There is strictly no admit-
tance, but two information and observation booths have been built around
the complex for visitors. These are accessible from Coal Mine Road and Camp
Street. One is located opposite the
entrance to the power station and the
other is 2km south west overlooking the
open cut coal mine.

The Anglesea River is the focal point
of the town and terminates in a small
lake before entering the ocean. It divides
the main hills on which the town is built
and provides flat land along its banks for
lawns, electric barbecues and recreation
space. A small jetty is a popular
launching spot for canoes and swimmers.

Anglesea is one of the few coastal
towns in the area to have retained its
sand dunes, and its gently shelved surf
beach provides both shallow water for
children and good board-riding and body
surfing waves. The area was originally
named Swampy Creek, but from 1885
was known as Anglesea River. In 1887
Anglesea House, later Anglesea Hotel,

was opened. The advent of the motor car brought the town closer to Geelong and Melbourne and since then its development as a holiday resort has been rapid.

Major Attractions

Anglesea is famous for its large population of kangaroos which graze the **Golf Course**. They can be seen at most times of the day, but are in larger numbers in the early morning and late afternoon. Turn right into Noble Street just over the bridge, then after 1km turn right again into Golf Links Road where the fairways can be seen separated by strips of native bush.

Coogoorah Park is located in bushland on the west side of the Anglesea River, a short walk from the bridge. Coogoorah is an Aboriginal name meaning swampy, reedy creek. The park has unique water ways and natural bush covered islands linked by a network of bridges and walkways. A flying fox suspended out over water is the feature of an adventure playground specially developed for children. Picnic facilities include electric barbecues, shelters and fresh water.

Take a stroll along the paths on Sanctuary Island through the magnificent bushland, native to the Anglesea area. Many plants have been named to increase your appreciation of the vegetation. The network of paths and bridges gives access to wetlands and reedbeds where native waterbirds congregate, especially early in the morning and at dusk. The waterways are also popular canoeing and fishing areas.

Trail rides through the Angahook-Lorne State Park in the hinterland surrounding Anglesea and Aireys Inlet can be arranged from Sea Mist Stud, 17 km north west of Anglesea. They can cater for the beginner or experienced rider for short treks or for several days with over night stays. Sea Mist also provides accommodation ranging from private to bunk rooms.

Anglesea is the gateway to some of the most spectacular stretches of coastal scenery in the world. The roadside lookout on the crest of a hill leaving

Grazing kangaroos at Anglesea Golf Course

Anglesea gives sweeping views to the east to steep, ochre-coloured cliffs and in the west to **Point Roadknight**, a popular family beach.

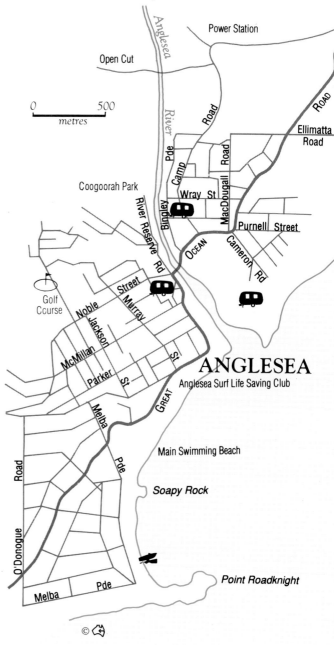

Anglesea beach and Point Roadknight

The Great Ocean Road from the Mornington Peninsula

Sorrento to Torquay
42 kilometres

Queenscliff Hotel lobby

A modern car and passenger ferry now makes it possible to reach the Great Ocean Road from the Mornington Peninsula via Sorrento and Queenscliff. The ferry provides a time saving option for both east- and west-bound motorists touring Victoria's coastline. It operates seven days a week with 12 crossings daily.

AT A GLANCE
QUEENSCLIFF
Distance:
103 km from Melbourne

Tourist Information:
A Maze'N Things
Cnr Bellarine Highway
and Grubb Road,
Wallington, Vic. 3221
Phone: (03) 5250 2669

Car & Pedestrian Ferries
*Peninsula Searoad Car &
Passenger Ferry-The
Peninsula Princess* is a
modern comfortable
vessel capable of
carrying 600 passengers
and 80 vehicles. The
crossing from Sorrento
to Queenscliff takes 40
minutes. You can watch
the scenery from the
decks or rest in the
lounge. You cannot
prebook so early arrival
is advised, particularly
for car transport.
Departs Sorrento Pier,
Nepean Highway, daily at
8am, 10am, 12noon, 2pm,
4pm, 6pm, and during
Summer, Friday & Sunday
only at 8pm. Departs
Queenscliff, Boat Harbour,
Larkin Street, at 7am, 9am,
11am, 1pm, 3pm, 5pm, and
during Summer, Friday &
Sunday only at 7pm.
24hr timetable information
(03) 5258 3244.

QUEENSCLIFF
Queenscliff is one of the best-preserved historic towns in Victoria. Overlooking Port Phillip Heads, it has quaint cottages and grand hotels marking the growth of over one hundred years as a fashionable seaside resort.

Bay steamers began plying the waters between Melbourne and Queenscliff during the 1850s, but it was not until the 1880s that it became a popular seaside resort. But Queenscliff's fame did not last, and for 50 years it slumbered as motor car ownership lured holiday-makers to more distant destinations. Fortunately the old buildings and fishing village atmosphere survived.

Queenscliff was reborn in the 1970s with the restoration of the grand hotels, guest-houses and other historic buildings. All development now is in sympathy with this unique Victorian town.

Major Attractions
Fort Queenscliff At the turn of the century Shortlands Bluff was the British Empire's most heavily-defended post south of the equator. It's giant cannons have been guarding the Heads since the 1880s when it was built to ward off a possible Russian invasion.

Within the Fort grounds is the Black Lighthouse, built in 1863 of bluestone quarried in Scotland, where the lighthouse column was erected, numbered, then dismantled and shipped to Australia. The only black lighthouse in Australia, mariners line it up with Queenscliff's white lighthouse forming a line by which they can steer safely through 'The Rip'. Also in this group of buildings is the stone Telegraph Station, built in 1863 during the Crimean War.

The Fort is now the home of the Australian Army Command Staff College.

You can explore the underground powder magazine and the Military Museum at the Fort on the daily guided tours. The educational and historical guided tours are conducted on weekdays 2pm only and weekends at 1pm and 3pm. Admission is charged.

Some **historic walks** will help you appreciate Queenscliff. Down Gellibrand Street are some magnificent buildings like '**Lathamstowe**', built in the 1880s by the founder of the Carlton Brewery as a gift to the Church of England. The **Ozone**, **Queenscliff** and **Esplanade**

QUEENSCLIFF

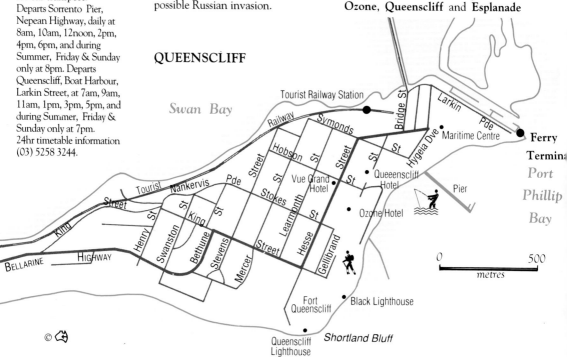

• THE BIG GUNS OF EARLY VICTORIA •

Queenscliffs' military connections date back to 1860 with the placement of three 68-pounder smooth bore muzzle loader cannons on the cliff top over looking 'The Rip'. Their placement was in response to fears of a Russian invasion.

In 1863 the 'black' and 'white' lighthouses were constructed. The black light is 39m above sea level and is constructed of bluestone, the white is 29m and constructed of timber and local stone.

In the early 1880s a municipal office block was built and in 1883 taken over by the army. A wall was built to enclose the buildings and the lighthouses. By 1884 it was completed along with its own 'keep' or watch-tower, and the Victorian Artillery was in residence. Three 9-inch guns were positioned.

Black lighthouse, wall and 'keep' at Fort Queenscliff

The walls are constructed of hand-made bricks with loopholes along its length. These are lined with iron and have vertical slits to fit rifle barrels. The 'keep' is the main watch-tower and gave excellent landward and seaward views in all directions. It originally had sleeping quarters on the first floor, and a storage space in the basement. It now houses a library.

In 1885 the Victorian Artillery Headquarters were moved from Melbourne to Queenscliff. By then 15 guns were in place; three 9-inch on platforms, one 6-inch in a pit,

one 80-pounder in a pit, three 80-pounders on platforms, one 8-inch in an open pit, two 40-pounders, two 6-pounders and two 10-barrel machine guns.

Some of these guns were known as 'Disappearing guns'. A hydro-pneumatic system used the gun's recoil energy to force the barrel down into a pit and out of sight for reloading. This meant that the gun was only exposed to the enemy for about 20 seconds at each firing.

Uniforms of the Victorian Artillery

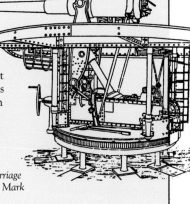
Drawing showing the Carriage and Disappearing 6 inch Mark II gun

Queenscliff's century-old **Railway Station** is the home of the **Bellarine Peninsula Railway**. A group of local rail enthusiasts operate the train, which take people around Swan Bay and across the high country to Drysdale. It is the longest 3'6" gauge tourist railway in Australia, with a large collection of locomotives and carriages, some dating back to the 1800s.

Sorrento-Portsea-Queenscliff Passenger Ferry Service
Daily service between the hours of 9am-5pm. Phone for timetable information on (03) 5984 1602 after 8am.

Hotels are also grand buildings. Hesse Street also has significant buildings including the **Vue Grand Guest-house** (1855-89) and on the opposite side of the street, the **Post Office** and **Library**. St George the Martyr **Anglican Church**, and the **Uniting Church** and Sunday school are also important.

Cliff-top walkways provide panoramic views of Bass Strait, the Mornington Peninsula and 'The Rip', the dangerous entrance to Port Phillip Bay, between Point Lonsdale and Port Nepean.

The **Queenscliff Historical Centre Museum**, Hesse Street (next to Post Office), houses a pictorial and relic collection covering the maritime and pioneering history of the area.

Bellarine Peninsula railway

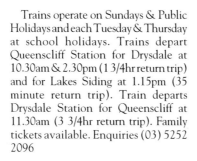

AT A GLANCE
Attractions:
Fort Queenscliff, Bellarine Peninsula Railway, Fishermans Wharf, Ocean View Lookout, Maritime Museum, Historic 19th Century hotels and Fishermans Cottages.

Accommodation:
3 Hotels
4 Caravan Parks
3 Guesthouses

Fishing:
Swan Bay Has long enjoyed the standing of the best whiting spot in Port Phillip. Good catches of Flathead, Salmon Trout, Pike and Mullet can be caught in their seasons.
Jetty: Some catches of Flathead and Mullet.

Bird watching:
Swan Island and surrounds: Pied Oystercatcher, Sharp-tailed Sandpiper, Red-necked Stint, Curlew Sandpiper, Grey, Lesser and Mongolian Plover, Ruddy Turnstone, Eastern Curlew and Red and Great Knot. Other waterbirds are; Australian Pelican, cormorants, Black-faced Shag, herons, egrets, ibis, gulls and terns. The best time for sighting migratory waders is December to February.

POINT LONSDALE
Distance:
99km from Melbourne

Accommodation:
2 Caravan Parks
2 Motels

Point Lonsdale Lighthouse

Trains operate on Sundays & Public Holidays and each Tuesday & Thursday at school holidays. Trains depart Queenscliff Station for Drysdale at 10.30am & 2.30pm (1 3/4hr return trip) and for Lakes Siding at 1.15pm (35 minute return trip). Train departs Drysdale Station for Queenscliff at 11.30am (3 3/4hr return trip). Family tickets available. Enquiries (03) 5252 2096

Fishermans Wharf is the colourful home of a small fleet of fishing vessels, the Port Phillip sea pilot's high-speed craft, the Marine Science Centre's research vessels and the Sorrento-Queenscliff car ferry.

Maritime Museum, is on the foreshore near the main pier. The fascinating maritime history of Port Phillip Heads is portrayed in the Maritime Centre, where the displays are arranged around Queenscliff's former life-boat used to carry out rescue missions in 'The Rip'. *Open:* Saturday and Sun. 1.30pm–4pm, school and public holidays 10.30am–4.30pm.

Adjacent to the Maritime Centre is the **Marine Science Centre**, where you can observe some of the coasts marine life close up.
Open: 10am–4pm all week and weekends in Janurary; during school holidays in April and September, and visits on request. Open to school groups throughout the year. Admission by donation. Phone (03) 5252 3344

Swan Island is controlled by the Australian Army and boasts a picturesque golf course which is open to the public. A trawler fleet anchors at 'The Creek' mooring between **Swan Island** and the township. **Swan Bay** stretching between Queenscliff and Edwards Point is a protected bay providing excellent fishing, boating and wind-surfing.

POINT LONSDALE
The township is perched on Port Phillip Heads, overlooking 'The Rip', one of the most treacherous seaways in the

Point Lonsdale Jetty

world. The entrance is only 1200m across and the tides flow through at 8 knots in a channel 15m deep, churning up turbulent water. Its lighthouse is a vital navigation aid to shipping.

Buckleys Cave Situated at the foot of the Point Lonsdale lighthouse, this cave was home to William Buckley, one of five convicts who escaped Victoria's first settlement at Sorrento in 1803. The luck of his survival is summed up in the old saying- 'You've got two chances - Buckley's, and none'.

Marconi Memorial This monument marks the site where in 1906 Marconi, the inventor of radio, made his first cross the sea broadcast from the mainland to Tasmania.

A Maze 'N Things Cnr Grubb Road and Bellarine Highway. Australia's largest three dimensional timber maze, with croquet lawn, golf putting green, children's playground and amazing holographics. It is also the Tourist Information Centre for the Bellarine Peninsula.

Moorfield Wildlife Park 400 Grubb Road, Wallington. First begun as a private deer farm, Moorfield Wildlife Park is in a bush setting with wildlife ranging from deer, kangaroos and wallabies, koalas and native birds.
Open: 10am–5pm daily Saturday to Thursday (Closed Friday, except during school holidays). Admission is charged.

OCEAN GROVE & BARWON HEADS
The twin holiday resorts of Ocean Grove and Barwon Heads are linked by a bridge over the Barwon River estuary. During the 1800s leather tanning was an important industry making use of the local forests of black wattles to provide bark for tanning.

Ocean Grove

Back in the 1850s Ocean Grove was settled by two American Wesleyan missionaries. They planned to establish an interdenominational settlement, like the one they had set up earlier at Ocean Grove in New Jersey. Their plan failed. However Ocean Grove evolved during the 1880s as a sanatorium for Methodist clergy and their congregations. The God-fearing pioneers placed a covenant on all land sales in the township prohibiting the manufacture and consumption of alcohol. To this day, there is no hotel in Ocean Grove.

A 6 km expanse of sandy beach between Ocean Grove and Barwon Heads, is one of Victoria's safest surfing beaches and provides facilities on the foreshore for 15 000 campers each summer. It has a very active surf club and State and National Surf Championships are held regularly.

Art and craft lovers will find much to entertain them at the town's two galleries and there are a host of pottery and craft shops.

Just north of the town is the **Ocean Grove Nature Reserve**, 143 hectares of natural bushland, the last large tract of timbered area on the Bellarine Peninsula. Walking tracks are sign-posted and plant species are named. The vegetation is dominated by gums, tea-tree, banksia, grass trees and orchids.

Koalas and other marsupials live in the reserve together with over 100 species of birds, including the rare pink robin and, of special scientific interest, two rare species of butterfly - the 'Fiery Jewel' and the 'Small Ant Blue'. Two hides are provided in the reserve for nature photographers, at the north waterhole and the west dam.

Barwon Heads is nestled at the mouth of the Barwon River and protected by the Bluff, a limestone headland. Surrounded on three sides by water, Barwon Heads is a wonderful place for water sports. Families have a long stretch of safe swimming beach on the river, sailors have a protected estuary for windsurfing or yachting. Surfers have kilometres of undeveloped coastline to explore and for divers there are many reefs and shipwrecks to explore.

Upstream on the Barwon River is **Lake Connewarre**, a shallow estuarine lagoon linked to Reedy Lake. There is an abundance of water-birds; especially at Reedy Lake, with its extensive reedbeds which provide shelter for water fowl. Lake Connewarre is ideal for small boats, yachting and fishing.

Just over the Bluff are rock pools, a protected shellfish habitat and the famous **13th Beach**, venue for surfing contests.

Terns and Silver Gulls at 13th Beach

Jirrahlinga Koala and Wildlife Sanctuary, Taits Road. A haven for kangaroos, wombats, koalas, echidnas, dingoes, reptiles and foxes as well as a variety of birds. It also has an animal nursery and hospital.
Open: Daily 10am-5pm. Phone (03)5254 2484. Admission is charged.

13th Beach

The construction of a bitumen road on the foredunes bordering 13th Beach has led to some erosion. Protective fencing has been constructed along the road to restrict pedestrian access to defined walkways in an effort to protect vegetation. In places the area looks a lot like a concentration camp, however the sand-dunes are gradually being stabilised and the road has opened up a spectacular stretch of ocean beach. Park at one of the wayside stops and walk down onto the wide beach for magnificent views back east to Barwon Heads and west to Torquay.

Breamlea

Breamlea is a quiet, secluded holiday town nestled in the sandhills adjacent to Bream Creek, between Barwon Heads and Torquay. A camping and caravan park with post office and store offers affordable family accommodation in a tranquil setting. A short walk over the sand dunes leads you onto the beautiful Bancoora Surf Beach. Keen surf fishermen will be rewarded with excellent catches.

Australian Pelican

Fishing:
Between Queenscliff and Pt Lonsdale:
Good medium sized Salmon, Salmon Trout, Flathead, and Mullet
Jetty: Flathead, Salmon Trout, Mullet.
Bass Strait: Salmon, Sharks, Ruff and Mullet. Yellowtail Kingfish are further off shore.

OCEAN GROVE
Distance:
103 km from Melbourne

Attractions:
Ocean Grove Nature Reserve, Ocean Grove Beach

Accommodation:
5 Caravan Parks
1 Hotel
4 Motels

BARWON HEADS
Distance:
95 km from Melbourne

Attractions:
The Bluff, 13th Beach, Lake Connewarre, Reedy Lake and Jirrahlinga Wildlife Sanctuary, Golf Course, Barwon Heads Village Park

Accommodation:
2 Caravan Parks
1 Hotel
1 Motel

Bird watching:
THE BLUFF
A good place to view seabirds; Wandering, Black-browed, Yellow-nosed and Shy Albatross, Cape and Great-winged Petrel, Slender-billed and Fairy Prion and Fluttering Shearwater.

LAKE CONNEWARRE
A vast wetland with stretches of open water, reedbeds and marshes has an abundance of waterbirds. Cormorants, herons, egrets, Little and Australian Bittern, Sacred and Straw-necked Ibis, spoonbills, waterfowl, Buff-banded and Lewin's Rail, Australian and Spotless Crake, Black-tailed Native-hen, Purple Swamphen, waders, Sharp-tailed Sandpiper, Painted Snipe, Marsh and Pectoral Sandpiper, gulls, and Whiskered and White-winged Tern (only in summer)

SPARKLING COAST AND HIDDEN WATERFALLS

ANGLESEA TO APOLLO BAY

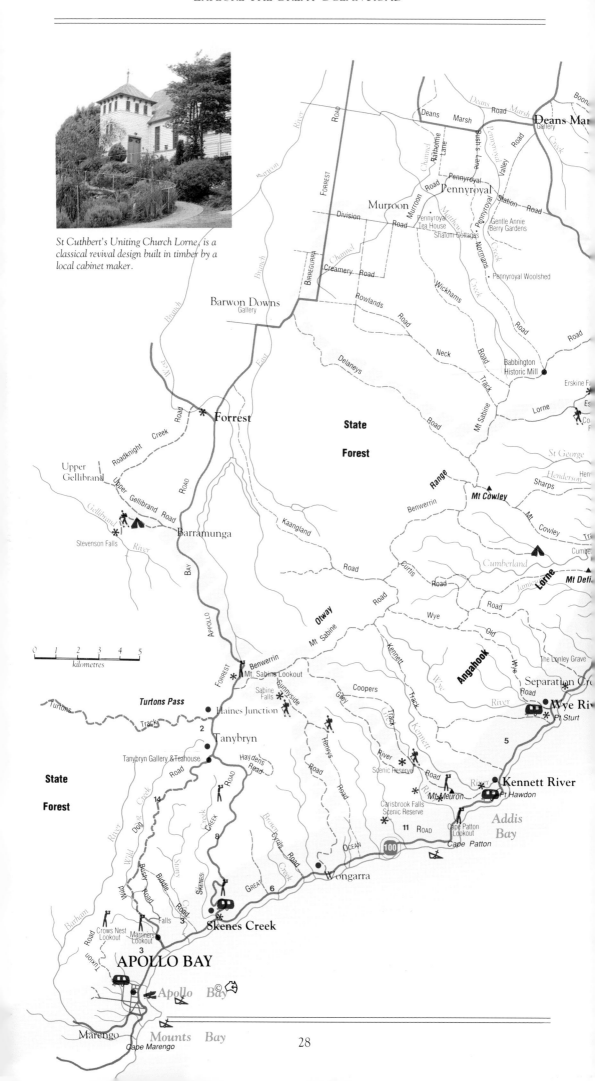

St Cuthbert's Uniting Church Lorne, is a classical revival design built in timber by a local cabinet maker.

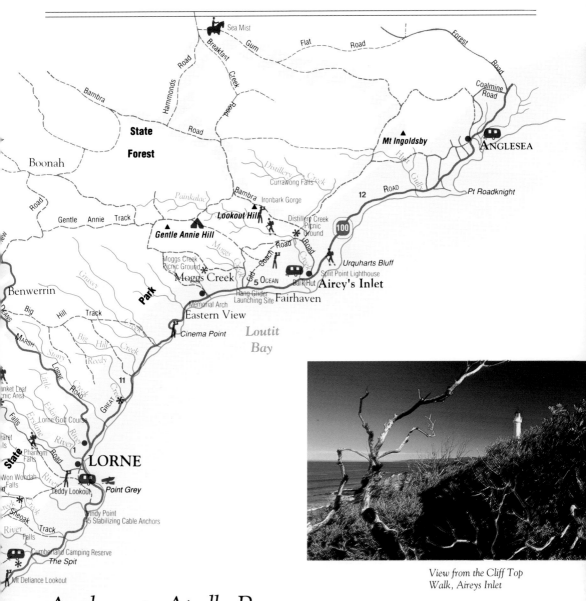

View from the Cliff Top
Walk, Aireys Inlet

PREVIOUS PAGES
The Great Ocean Road
clings to the cliffs between
Aireys Inlet and Lorne.

Anglesea to Apollo Bay
74 kilometres

As you leave Anglesea and cross the ridge that ends abruptly at Point
Roadknight, a long sweeping surf beach comes into view. In the distance the
beach meets the block-like headlands of Urquhart Bluff and further on to
Aireys Inlet where the lighthouse is visible on the horizon. Undersea
volcanoes helped create the rocky cliffs and stacks along the coast at Aireys
Inlet. Walking tracks from Distillery and Moggs Creeks picnic areas lead you
inland into the ironbark forests of the Angahook-Lorne State Park.

The Memorial Arch at Ocean View marks the beginning of the Great Ocean
Road, cut out of the cliff faces of the Otway Ranges which run along the coast
to Apollo Bay. The road twists, climbs, crosses fast flowing streams, but never
leaves the ocean and provides a succession of sparkling seascapes. No matter
what time of the year, or weather, this section of coastline is always spectacular.

Deep in the rainforests behind Lorne waterfalls like Erskine, Phantom,
Kalimna and Cora Lynn have been perfect destinations for a bush walk or
picnic for generations. The Lonely Grave next to the Great Ocean Road just
beyond Artillery Rocks is testimony to the lost lives in the many shipwrecks in
the early pioneering days.

At Cape Patton the forest gives way to rolling farmland as you look west to
Apollo Bay. Carisbrook Falls just west of the Cape are the highest waterfalls
along the coast. Take time to stop and explore the waterfalls, cascades and
rapids that drop over 200m in less than half a kilometre.

Aireys Inlet

Sea Star, Aireys Inlet beach

'White Lady' lighthouse on Split Point

Aireys Inlet is the place where the cliffs meet the ocean and the forest meets the sand. Locals say the rock pools beneath the cliffs create some of the best swimming spots and places to beachcomb in the area. **Steps Beach** is the pick of the bunch. **Gully Beach** is another popular spot and is rarely crowded. To get to Gully Beach you turn down Eagle Rock Parade from the Great Ocean Road, then turn into Alice Street. The beach is only a short walk away.

Aireys Inlet is named after an early squatter, John Eyrie, who settled there in 1842. For many years the settlement was the terminus of the Cobb and Co. coastal coach service from Geelong. The town developed slowly after the building of the lighthouse in 1891.

The Bark Hut is a replica of a settlers' hut built in 1852 from timber, bark and bricks. It is a copy of the residence of Thomas and Martha Pearce who died in 1862 and 1870. Their graves are on the cliff top near the lighthouse where a cairn marks the site.

The hut survived until 1979 when the National Trust and Shire of Barrabool funded its restoration, however it was destroyed during the Ash Wednesday wild fires in February 1983. The descendants of Thomas Pearce rebuilt the hut to original specifications in 1985.

Split Point Lighthouse is locally known as the 'white lady' and it's fully automatic light is visible for 30 km to sea, and it plays an important role in directing shipping towards the lighthouses on Port Phillip Heads. From the sea the rock looks as though it has split away. Park the car and take the short walk to the end of the headland for a fine view of Aireys Inlet beach and the surround-

AT A GLANCE
AIREYS INLET
Distance:
119km from Melbourne

Picnic Spots:
Moggs Creek Located in the Lorne/Angahook State Park
Distillery Creek Turn right into Bambra Road and continue for 3km.

Places to visit:
Split Point Lighthouse
The Bark Hut

Accommodation:
1 Motel
1 Caravan Park

Bird watching:
Aireys Inlet supports some waterbirds such as; herons, ibis, grebes, swans and few duck, but upstream in the swamp habitat, Moorhen.

The rebuilt Bark Hut

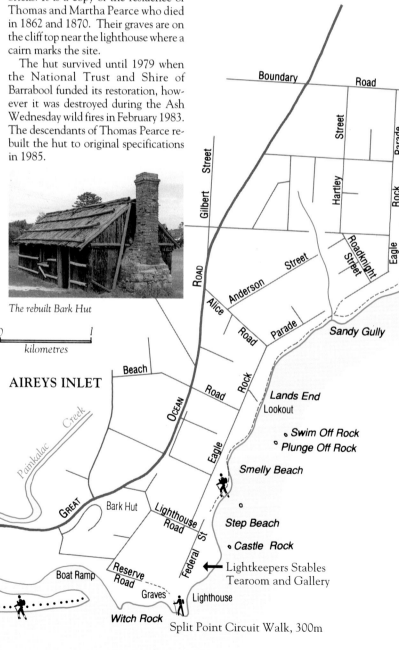

ing Otway Ranges, and catch a glimpse of the fur seals that sometimes rest on the rocks below.

Aireys Inlet to Moggs Creek Walk
(Section of the Surf Coast Walk)
Distance: 10km *Time:* 4 hours
Grade: easy–medium
This walk is one of the most interesting sections of the Surf Coast Walk and follows the cliff tops from Boundary Road passing Eagle Rock and the lighthouse. Cross the estuary of Painkalac Creek and walk west along the wide surf beach to Fairhaven. From the Fairhaven Surf Club the track leaves the beach and takes you back into the Angahook State Park. The track climbs up a ridge line and cuts the Moggs Creek Lookout track. The 2km return diversion will reward you with 360° views from the lookout. From the ridge line the **Surf Coast Walking Track** descends

Eagle Rock off Split Point

down to Old Coach Road. A left turn at this point and another 200m, then a right takes you onto Gentle Annie Track. Its a steady climb up Gentle Annie Track for about 1km where an unnamed track leads south to Moggs Creek Picnic Area, the finish of the Surf Coast Walk.

Swamphen, Banded Landrail, Japanese Snipe, grassbirds and White-fronted Chats are present. Rufous Bristlebirds, Singing, Yellow-winged, and White-eared Honeyeaters, Wattlebirds and Silver eyes are common in the coastal scrub. The coastal forest contains parrots, lorikeets, honeyeaters, Eastern Spinebills (the honeyeaters are especially common when the red ironbark is in flower) and many insectivores. The Brown Goshawk, Collared Sparrowhawk, Peregrine and Little Falcon and Powerful Owls are also present.

• VOLCANOES ALONG THE BEACH •

The remains of the submarine volcanoes that produced ash and 'bombs' (once molten lumps of lava shot from the exploding volcano) can be seen near Aireys Inlet. From the vantage point of the lighthouse, at the end of Federation Street at Split Point, you can see two stacks out to sea. Eagle Rock is to the east and Table Rock to the south. These two remnants are made up of a yellowish limestone filled with marine invertebrate fossils. It forms a 20m layer at the top of the stacks. Below this lies the dark coloured remains of lava flows (basalts), and a variety of other volcanic materials, deposited as air fall material; water and wind as it flowed down the volcanic cone. The eruption originated on the sea floor and built it's cone up to sea-level and above.

sea at the time when Australia and Antarctica finally separated about 35 million years ago. Out in the surf you will see some dark black rocks of the shore platform. These are the basalts of ancient lava flows that once covered the ocean floor. In some places marine invertebrate fossils can be seen where the living organisms must have attached themselves to the cooled sea floor. In other places the basalts seem to have injected themselves into the marine sediments being deposited at the time.

To the east of Aireys Inlet at the end of Boundary Road is a long path that goes down to the sea. It is worth the hike down through the seaside vegetation. At the eastern end of the beach you will see the remains of violent volcanic activity. Much of the material preserved in the cliffs and in the headland is airfall volcanic material. Fine-grained ash and dark basaltic volcanic bombs are distributed randomly through the coastal cliff face. This volcano blew it's top some 35-36 million years ago.

Basalt 'bombs' on the shore platform

Basalt overlain with sandstone at Split Point

If you are interested in fossils, walk down to the beach that is to the west of Split Point, just below the lighthouse. The path is lined with big blocks of Point Addis Limestone which reveals a variety of fossils of the moss-like bryozoans, sea urchins (echinoids) and clams. These fossils are of forms that lived in a shallow

Volcanic vent on the waters edge, off Boundary Road

Angahook–Lorne State Park

AT A GLANCE
Ranger-In-Charge
Anglesea Work Centre
Harvey Street,
Anglesea Vic 3230
Phone : (03)5263 3144

Lorne Work Centre
86 Polwarth Road
Lorne 3232
Phone: (03) 5289 1732

Camping: Allenvale, Off
Sharps Track near
Sheoak Picnic Reserve.

The 22 350 ha park was declared in 1987. It stretches from Aireys Inlet to Kennett River along the spine of the Otway Ranges. The park contains some of the finest coastal and timbered hill country in Victoria. Along the coast, cliffs reach 100m above the ocean and are interspersed with small coves, sandy beaches and wide rock platforms. The ridges of the Otways rise steeply from the coast, separating deep valleys where fast flowing streams have cut spectacular gorges with waterfalls and cascades.

Currawong Falls

Vegetation ranges from low heathland to towering forests. Because of the large variations in rainfall, soil type, altitude and proximity to the sea the Angahook-Lorne park has a great diversity of plant life. The drier section of the park around Aireys Inlet with only 650mm of annual rainfall supports heathlands, orchids, bush and parrot peas, hakeas, grass trees, tea-trees, sheoaks and hibbertias. During spring and early winter, Iron Bark Gully, Distillery Creek and Moggs Creek are a blaze of colour.

Another feature of the park are the paperbark swamps lining Distillery and Salt Creeks. Scented paperbark grows in dense thickets in association with coral fern and tea-tree.

In the wetter and steeper sections of the park between Lorne and Cape Patton dense rainforests clad the range. Here the 1000mm of annual rainfall supports towering blue gum, mountain ash, messmate, and mountain grey gum.

Distillery Creek Picnic Ground
Turn right into Bambra Road and travel 3km to Distillery Creek picnic ground in the Angahook-Lorne State Park. Picnic tables and barbecues are scattered through bushland on both sides of Bambra Road, however the toilets for the disabled and information board are located in the southern section of the reserve. The reserve is the starting point for a network of walking tracks into Ironbark Gorge and Currawong Falls.

Distillery Creek Nature Trail
Distance: 1.7 km *Time:* 35 minutes return *Grade:* easy
A short nature trail shows a diversity of plant life.

Currawong Falls Walk
Distance: 12 km *Time:* 4 hours return
Grade: easy–medium
Distillery Creek has cut a notch through a jagged rock shelf which overhangs a beautiful fern gully. The **Currawong Falls** look like a horses tail as the water jets over the rock ledge and is broken into a fine mist before reaching the pools below. The falls and surrounding outcrops are more like the arid gorge scenery of Central Australia than a waterfall in the Otways.

The Currawong Falls Walk is well signposted and starts at the Distillery Creek Picnic Reserve. It is best to walk the track in a clockwise direction to make the most of the spectacular views along the way. Cross the Bambra Road and pick up the Ironbark Gorge track to where the Currawong Falls Track is indicated climbing up onto a high plateau above the cliffs of the Ironbark Gorge. Continue over the plateau towards the Trig Point before crossing Loves Track. At this point you can see the Alcoa Power Station and the lighthouse at Aireys Inlet. After reaching this high point the track swings in a westerly direction heading down into Distillery Creek. Once you reach Distillery Creek the track swing east towards Currawong Falls. The track crosses the creek 200m above the falls. This is a beautiful place to have lunch. Many have taken shelter below the falls under the overhanging rock face when caught in a shower of rain.

Head down the valley away from the falls until the track swings north into a small side gully. During winter a small cascade is formed before the track rejoins Distillery Creek and enters a fern grove. Another 500m along the track it skirts

Cycling The Great Ocean Road

a paperbark swamp which is brimming with bird life. The track follows the western bank of Distillery Creek before emerging onto Bambra Road. Walk west along Bambra Road and you will pick up a small side track which will take you back into Distillery Creek Picnic Reserve.

Ironbark Gorge Walk

Distance: 5km   *Time:* 2 hours return
Grade: easy

This walk offers panoramic views along Ironbark Gorge and cuts through stands of red ironbark and dry open forest where pink heath and the hooded green orchid can be seen in flower from early spring through to October.

From the Distillery Creek car-park cross Bambra Road through a small picnic area and follow the lower track along the gully. Keep bearing left. Do not take the higher track which leads to the Currawong Falls. The track crosses the creek several times before reaching the upper reaches of the gorge. Here a sheer cliff face rises about 25m on the eastern side of the stream before the track swings sharply to the south east and begins to climb steeply out of the gorge. The track then follows the contours back into the Distillery Creek picnic area.

Angahook Forest Drive

Distance: 50km   *Time:* 3 hours.

The drive begins at Distillery Creek Picnic Ground and allows the visitor to see the impact of wildfires and rejuvenation processes at work in the Australian bush.

On Ash Wednesday, 16 February 1983, a fire started near Deans Marsh 20km west. High temperatures and gale-force northerly winds drove it into Lorne in 45 minutes. A westerly wind change then fanned the fire towards Anglesea, burning 41 000 hectares of mostly-forested land, as well as destroying over 700 houses and claiming three lives.

The Australian bush has evolved with drought and fire as part of the environment and has developed ways of surviving these natural events. During this drive you will see some of the effects of the fire on the forest and some of nature's adaptations to fire.

Stop 1 *Distillery Creek Picnic Ground - Bambra - Aireys Inlet Road*
This area was only lightly burnt. Shrubs have since recolonised the area with thickets of dogwood, hakea and young seedlings of red ironbark.

Stop 2 *Waterhole - 4.5km from Start of Bambra Road*
The trees in this particular area were more severely burnt and some killed by the fire. Looking around you can see signs of the bush recovering.

Stop 3 *Peters Hill Fire Tower - 6.4km from Stop 2 on Bambra Road*
A fire storm raced through the tree tops in this area which was followed some time later by a ground fire. You can see that the ground fire was not hot enough to burn the sign in front of the tower and yet the heat from the crown fire was so intense that it burnt the cabin on the tower which was 24m above the ground.

Stop 4 *Junction of Boonah Road - 0.4km from Tower*
From here you can see the remains of a pine plantation, 770 hectares of it was completely destroyed by the fire. This timber would have had a value of over $4.5 million in 20 years time. The plantation has since been replanted with radiata pine.

Stop 5 *Back track past the Tower and turn left into Hammond Road - 7.2km*
The fire crossed the road from left to right (i.e. from west to east) and was so intense on the left-hand side of the road that the tops of the trees were completely burnt. On the right-hand side of the road, the fire was milder due to a change in aspect and the reduced combustible fuel provided by the road.

Stop 6 *Gum Flat Road - 5.5km from Stop 5 to main gate into International Harvester's Proving Ground.*
'Cool burns' were carried out in this area over many years which meant there was a reduction in the amount of combustible material on the forest floor. The fire did not create as much fierce heat which probably accounted for the installations in the proving grounds not being destroyed.

Stop 7 *Bald Hills Road - 5.1km from Stop 6*
You are now overlooking heathlands to the north of Anglesea. The patches of green are the result of past cool burns. This area in spring becomes a glorious carpet of wildflowers and orchids which have been stimulated to flower by the fire.

From Stop 7 on *Bald Hills Road* continue along No2 Road then left into Distillery Creek Road back to Distillery Creek picnic area. The final leg of the drive is through heathland.

Commemorative plaques

Fairhaven

A short distance beyond Aireys Inlet is Fairhaven, site of the Surf Life Saving Club. Public toilets are located beside the road.

Views to the west are of Fairhaven and Eastern View surf beaches, and to the town of Lorne-on the distant headland.

Moggs Creek

This is a small holiday resort situated at the mouth of Moggs Creek overlooking a magnificent surf beach. Tucked away in native bush behind the town is **Moggs Creek Picnic Reserve**. There are individual wood barbecue and picnic tables scattered amongst ironbark gums. The reserve is reached by turning north into Old Coach Road and left into Boyd Avenue.

Moggs Creek Coastal View Walk

Distance: 6km *Time:* 1.5 hours return
Grade: easy–medium
Leaving Moggs Creek Picnic Reserve you can take a short walk in a north west direction where you meet the lower track of the circuit which winds through dry forest and heathland in a south west direction to meet Moggs Creek Track. Cross the track and continue to a vantage point above a small cliff overlooking the coast. The unbroken view stretches from Aireys Inlet in the east to the Memorial Arch in the west. Retrace your steps to Moggs Creek Track and follow it west for 200m where the return circuit track is sign posted back to Moggs Creek. The well-sheltered walk will show you a diverse range of bird and plant life.

Moggs Creek Lookout The lookout gives 360° views of the Anglahook Park, Peters Hill, which can be identified by the fire tower on it's summit, east towards Aireys Inlet and south west to Lorne. The view is a spectacular sight at night with the periodic flashes from lighthouses, and ships at sea. The track to the lookout runs east off the Old Coach Road 200m north of the intersection of Gentle Annie Track. It is sandy and steep but can be negotiated in a conventional vehicle or will make a pleasant 3km return walk.

A **Hang Glider Launching Site** is located above the Great Ocean Road east of Moggs Creek. On most days during the summer you can watch gliders sweep out over the surf and ride the updrafts along the coastal slopes. A favourite landing spot for beginners is the wide surf beach at the mouth of Moggs Creek.

Eastern View

The Memorial Archway, Eastern View, signals the start of the Great Ocean Road, a magnificent memorial to those who served Australia during World War

Ocean View buildings near the Memorial Arch

One. The idea of a road to link the isolated south-coast towns was a vision of Mr W Calder, Chairman of the Country Roads Board of Victoria. He also saw its construction as a way to employ returned servicemen.

Horses and men battled the Southern Ocean weather and the rain sodden bushland of the Otway Ranges until the road's completion in 1932. It was a spectacular feat of engineering considering the lack of modern earth-moving equipment. The road is now one of the great coastal routes of the world.

Grassy Creek was the site of one of the major work camps during the construction of the Great Ocean Road. The first toll gate was located on the road between Grassy Creek and the Devil's Elbow. Secluded rock pools and cascades are situated a short distance upstream from the mouth of Grassy Creek and were a favourite bathing spot for the weary ex-soldiers after an exhausting day on the road works.

Cinema Point Lookout, provides an excellent view over Grassy Creek to Eastern View and Fairhaven surf beach.

Lorne

Lorne has been a favourite destination for holiday makers for generations. Rambling guest houses, modern holiday flats, and the serrated roof line of the Cumberland Resort blend into the tree tops of the huge gums which stretch from the forest behind, down to the main street. Across the road, parks, tennis courts, bowling greens, swimming pools and the surf club have been landscaped along the foredune of Victoria's best known and safest surf beach. Lorne, nestled around the mouth of the Erskine River, between two headlands of the Otway Ranges, is largely protected from the Southern Ocean weather.

Lorne has something for everyone, a variety of accommodation, restaurants and one of Victoria's best coastal shopping centres, plus the natural attractions of sun, sand, surf and bush. In January each year it hosts the famous *Pier to Pub Swim*, an event which attracts swimmers from all over Australia. In May, *The Otway Classic Foot Race* attracts international competitors who are challenged by the gruelling hills of the Otway Ranges surrounding Lorne. The main street, Mountjoy Parade is named after the Mountjoy brothers who in 1868 hand built the original Eskine House. Some years later they pioneered a coach service from Lorne over the rugged Otways to Winchelsea. Lorne serves as an ideal base to explore the wonderful hinterland of the Angahook-Lorne State Park. The park contains over 100 kilometres of walking tracks and beautiful waterfalls, including Erskine, Splitters, Won Wondah, Phantom and Kalimna. The Cora Lynn Cascades walk is one of the most scenic, taking in a narrow canyon where Cora Lyn Creek cascades over exposed shale ledges below huge tree ferns and towering trees.

AT A GLANCE
LORNE
Distance:
137 km from Melbourne

Tourist Information
Surf Coast Shire
Information Centre
144 Mountjoy Parade
Lorne 3132
Phone (03) 5289 1152

Department of Natural
Resources & Environment
Lorne Work Centre
86 Polwarth Road
Lorne 3232
Phone: (03) 5289 1732

Accommodation:
6 Motels
1 Hotel
2 Hotel/Motels
6 Caravan Parks
2 Guest Houses
3 Holiday Flats

Picnic Spots:
Teddy Lookout off
George St,
Blanket Leaf Picnic Area off
Erskine Falls Rd and *Sheoak Picnic Area*, beyond
Allenvale.

Fishing:
Lorne Pier Whiting,
Barracouta and Trevally are
common catches.
Rivers Trout and Bream
can be caught in the
Erskine, St George and
nearby rivers.
Rocks & Surf Salmon,
Snapper and Garfish are
caught from the rocks and
surf beaches.

The breathtaking coastal scenery on the approach to Lorne.

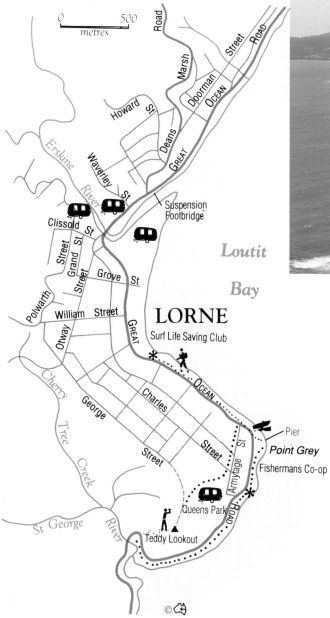

Looking towards Lorne from Cinema Point.

View across Loutit Bay to Lorne and The Cumberland.

The bay was named after Captain Loutit, who sought shelter around 1846 while retrieving cargo from a shipwreck. It was first settled by William Lindsay, a timber-cutter who began tree felling in the area. Subdivision began in 1869 when the town was named after the Marquis of Lorne. Much of its colourful history is preserved in the gracious homes which remain.

The opening of the Great Ocean Road in 1932 brought the holiday makers who turned the town into one of Victoria's premier tourist destinations.

Erskine Falls is a worthwhile detour when enjoying the Great Ocean Road scenery near Lorne. Located a few kilometres inland, along a mostly sealed road, the falls cascade over one of the highest drops in the Otway Ranges. They are quite spectacular. A viewing platform has been built overlooking the falls. Especially built steps have been constructed all the way down to the base of the falls for another view.

Lorne Golf Course runs along the ridge behind the township off Deans Marsh Road. It also gives a view over Loutit Bay which is particularly attractive in the late afternoon when the sun backlights the pier.

Short Walks around Lorne Township
Teddy Lookout Walk
via Armytage Street.
Distance: 3km *Time:* 2 hours return
Grade : medium
Set out from the Pacific Hotel, opposite the Lorne Pier and walk up Armytage Street into Queens Park. A lookout is situated in Queens Park where there is a picnic shelter and tables scattered amongst trees overlooking Loutit Bay. Wallabies from the surrounding bush graze in the park in the early mornings and at dusk. The lookout is 50m from the car-park and gives spectacular views over the mouth of the St George River and the Great Ocean Road benched into the cliff faces below. A brass plaque commemorates Lornes' Centenary in 1988 and shows distances to coastal and inland features.

From Teddy Lookout take the zig-zag track to the St George River Bridge and return to Lorne along the Great Ocean Road, where you can visit the tea rooms on your way back to the pier.

Erskine Valley Walk
Distance: 2km return *Time:* 1 hour
Grade: easy
A walk upstream through Erskine River Caravan Park takes you to the Rapids and Sanctuary.
The Sanctuary is a natural rock amphitheatre located 600m upstream from the caravan park. This place was used by visiting clergymen from 1850-1875 to conduct church services, prior to the first church being built at Lorne in 1875.

Day Walks around Lorne
Erskine Falls Walk
Distance: 7.5km *Time* : 4 hours each way *Grade* : medium

Start from either the Erskine River Caravan Park or from the Erskine Falls Road car-park.

Framed by tall tree-ferns, **Erskine Falls** are considered the best in the Lorne district, whatever the volume of water spilling over the ledge at the top of the falls. During the summer months a narrow shoot breaks into a curtain of spray as it falls from ledges covered with bright green moss. After heavy rains the mood changes and the river gushes straight down onto rocks at the base.

There are a number of fords to be negotiated along the length of the track, with some fords providing fairly safe crossings. The track twists and turns in places, sometimes following a course at river level, elsewhere climbing high to avoid particularly thick scrub or large rock bluffs. During the winter months the track is wet and slippery. Negotiate the natural bridges above the stream with care. Do not attempt crossings when water levels are high.

Erskine River footbridge

Straw Falls are a 15m cascade pouring into the Erskine River from its northern bank approximately 400m downstream from the Erskine Falls.

There is a viewing platform located just off the track with views across to Splitters Falls.

The Sanctuary is the natural rock amphitheatre located 1km upstream from the Erskine River Caravan Park.

In gullies along tributary creeks, and along the Erskine River valley itself, tree-ferns, hazel, water-ferns and blackwood grow in luxuriant profusion together with bush peas, goodenia and sweet bursaria. The balm mint bush gives off its distinctive strong perfume

Erskine Falls are awesome when in full flood.

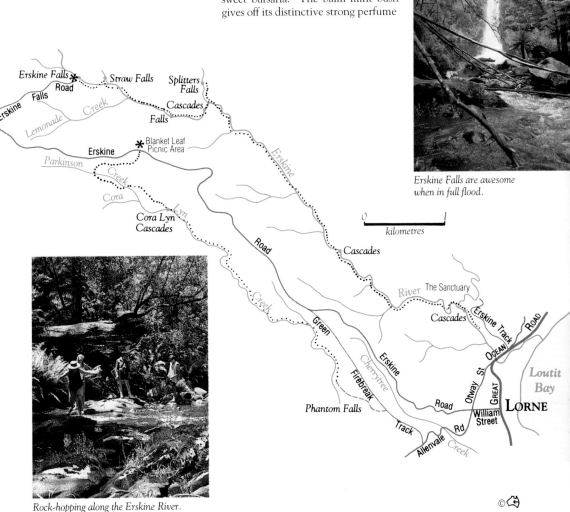

Rock-hopping along the Erskine River.

One of the many spurs of The Great Ocean Road

The Grand Pacific Hotel, Lorne, photographed in the 1900s. The gothic style building still stands minus the tower and wrought iron.

Kookaburras are always present at Sheoak Picnic Ground.

when in flower during spring along the track. On the spurs, the forest consists of mountain ash, tall blue gum and manna gum, with an understorey of black wattle, maiden hair fern and Australian clematis.

Cora Lynn Cascades Walk
Distance: 6km one way *Time :* 2.5 hrs
Grade: medium
This is one of the most scenic walks in the Lorne-Angahook Forest Park. The track was reconstructed in 1981 and now leads you on a relatively easy walk, but after heavy rain the section through the gorge can be slippery.

The walk can either be begun at Blanket Leaf Picnic Area or Cora Lynn car-park. Starting at the Blanket Leaf Picnic Area however gives you a gentle down hill descent all the way to Cora Lynn car-park.

Cora Lynn Cascades. The Cora Lynn Creek rises from a permanent spring further up the mountain, and cascades over a series of exposed shale ledges. Immediately below the cascades the track takes you rock-hopping through a gorge for a short distance. This canyon was formed as the Cora Lynn Creek eroded through the soft shales, providing cool, moist recesses for pockets of ferns and lichens.

The track down stream from the cascades follows the creek and makes numerous creek crossings, the perfect way to cool your feet in the summer.

On the track down from Blanket Leaf Picnic Area to the cascades, blue gum and messmate stringybark predominate with a varied understorey of mint bush, hazel, Austral mulberry, prickly currant-bush and blanketwood.

Sheoak Picnic Ground is a tranquil spot nestled amongst towering gums next to the tree-fern-lined banks of Sheoak Creek. Tables, wood barbecues, shelters and toilets are provided. Numerous walking tracks radiate out from here.

Allen Dam-Canyon Circuit Walk
including: Allenvale, Phantom, Henderson and Won Wondah Falls
Distance: 10km *Time:* 5 hours
Grade: easy
You can leave the Sheoak Picnic Ground and head north over Sheoak Creek up onto the Allenvale Road. The little settlement of Allenvale is 2km further on to the right. Cross the bridge over the St George River at Allenvale and head up the hill for 200m towards Lorne where a track is signposted to Phantom Falls on your left.

The pathway skirts private land and continues upstream in a north westerly direction through manna and blue gums with messmate stringybarks on the higher slopes. The track hugs the south bank of the St George River before crossing a small foot bridge. At this

point the track leaves the St George River and follows the Cora Lynn Creek upstream to the Cora Lynn car-park.

From the car-park take the Henderson Track and follow it north west for 300m where the track turns south west to take you to **Allen Dam**. This is a small tranquil reservoir, a great place to take a rest.. From the dam the track takes you down to the **Phantom Falls**. You can reach the base of the falls via a small path on the east side of the river. Phantom Falls is a15m sheer drop from a rock ledge to a large pool below.

Henderson Track then swings away from the falls and around a minor spur before reaching the **Canyon**. At the Canyon the track drops into a large pot hole then takes you through an arch forming the entrance to the Canyon. Here sheer walls rise 10m from the creek bed. Caves are dotted along the walls, but need some diligence to find. In spring the green hooded orchids flower in the damp recesses of the canyon.

From the Canyon the track swings sharply in a southerly direction through a fern glade down to Henderson Creek. From here the track swings west. A side track is signposted to **Henderson Falls** and runs up through a dense hazel and blackwood forest to the falls. The shining black rock face of the falls contrasts vividly with the clinging moss and overhanging vegetation. This is a great place to rest and enjoy the peace and beauty. Retrace your steps to the main track and follow it east to Won Wondah Falls

Won Wondah Falls are a pretty cascade, flowing between low rock walls, partly shrouded by overhanging ferns. From the falls it is an easy walk back to the Sheoak Picnic Area.

Kalimna Falls Walk
Distance: 8km return *Time:* 4 hours
Grade: easy
Two paths leave Sheoak Picnic Ground to take you to Kalimna Falls. The Upper Track follows the original timber tramway on the north side of Sheoak Creek. The Lower Track runs along the south side of Sheoak Creek. Both tracks meet about 1.5km upstream.

The Upper Kalimna track is signposted on the opposite side of the road to the picnic ground. Continue along the even graded tramway for 1.5km until the Lower Kalimna Tack joins.

Along the path are the **Lower Kalimna Falls.** You can walk behind the curtain of water of the 3m falls into a grotto. Through the curtain of water you can see a large pool reflecting the surrounding tree ferns.

The Upper **Kalimna Falls** are a further 1km upstream. They are a series of rock ledges which break the main stream into a series of small shoots, tumbling from one level to the next down a 20m

Lower Kalimna Falls

drop. Retrace your steps back to the track junction past the Lower Kalimna Falls and take the alternative track back to the Sheoak Picnic Ground.

Scenic Drive:
Lorne–Erskine Falls–Pennyroyal Valley
Distance: 65km *Time:* Half a day
Leave Lorne via William Street which becomes Erskine Falls Road.

Blanket Leaf Picnic Area is one of the most popular places for a barbecue around Lorne. It is also the starting point for the Cora Lynn Cascades walking track. It has a picnic shelter, fresh water, barbecue facilities and toilets, including those for the disabled.

The famous **Erskine Falls** have been featured in honeymoon photographs since the turn of the century. They have a spectacular 30m drop into a tree-fern-lined pool below. Erskine Falls Road goes within 80m of the falls. A short walk leads to a viewing platform. For the more adventurous, a new pathway has been constructed down the steep valley to take you to the spectacular fern gully at the base of the falls. Seats have been built so you can rest and catch your breath on the way back up.

Delaneys is a well-formed gravel road winding through the Otway State Forests towering gums and shaded fern gullies. Care should be taken during the winter months as sections of the road become slippery after heavy rain.

Division Road is the gateway to the Pennyroyal Valley with its tea-houses, 'pick-your-own' berry farms and local crafts.

Pennyroyal Tea House and Herb Garden on Division Road, offers raspberries and blackberries for picking from early summer through to the autumn. Attentive staff will bake scones to order while you wander through the herb garden, breathe in the lavender or inspect locally-woven cane baskets and bush furniture.
Open: December–February 11am-5pm (closed Tuesday)

Pennyroyal Woolshed is filled with crafts, home-made goods and nicknacks, including the occasional litter of Jack Russell puppies. It is situated on Nelson's farm at the end of Normans Road. The spectacular view from the woolshed must have been a distraction to the shearing teams of old. You look over the basalt plains to Birregurra and south over pine plantations on the northern slopes of the Otway Ranges. Beside the woolshed are some farm yard animals, waiting to be fed. The crafts include local hand-knitted jumpers and embroidery.
Open: December–February 10am-6pm. Then every weekend, school and public holidays.

Gentle Annie Berry Gardens have re-kindled an old tradition of berry growing in the Pennyroyal Valley once famous for its fruit. They have combined it with home cooking and country hospitality. Many Lorne regulars will remember the beautiful berry fruit produced at 'Gentle Annie' when it was situated beside the river at Allenvale. Their new berry gardens in the Pennyroyal Valley are still a great place to fill up containers with fresh berry fruit: strawberries, raspberries, blueberries and black currants.
Open: November–May 10am–6pm (closed Wednesday).

Sheoak Falls and Swallow Cave Walk
Distance: 2km *Time:* 1 hour each way *Grade:* easy
Drive to the car-park at the mouth of Sheoak River on the Great Ocean Road. Sheoak Falls is 300m from the Great Ocean Road car-park.
Swallow Cave is a shallow cave carved from the soft shale by the Sheoak Creek. Large numbers of 'tree martin' swallows nest in the roof crevices each spring.

Kalimna walking track between the upper and lower falls.

Raspberry picking at Gentle Annie Berry Gardens.

• BOLTING BACK A MOUNTAIN •

The Otway Ranges are composed for the most part of Cretaceous age sandstones with interbedded mudstone. Bedding planes are obvious, and in many places where they dip towards the road have brought about landslides which have plagued the Great Ocean Road for decades.

The worst of these developed at Windy Point 3km west of Lorne. The unstable rock extends 70m above the road, and is easily seen on the bare cliffs. Windy Point has a natural tendency toward rock slides, with bedding planes dipping at 27° toward the ocean, and include at least two beds of unstable mudstone. In 1968, minor road works cut into the toe of the hillside and triggered a slide of 200 000 tonnes. It developed slowly at first over two winters until finally heavy rains increased the movement to 2cm a day and a 3000 tonne rock landed on the road.

Closure of the road for six months in 1971 nearly isolated the small holiday settlements of Cumberland and Wye Rivers and restricted access to Apollo Bay further west.

The slide continuing to move every time there was heavy rain, and fissures 15m deep opened up in just two weeks. The options to make the road safe were limited: until engineers Adrian Williams, Lance Endersbee with geologist Alan Muir, found a solution to stabilise the slide with cable anchors.

Drilling rigs were suspended over the steep rock faces and holes drilled into the stable rock, 43m below. Thick metal cables were threaded into the bore holes, anchored and capped on the surface, locking the entire rock slide.

The tops of the 45 anchors can be seen dotted around the slide. Altogether they exert a stabilising force of 7700 tonnes.

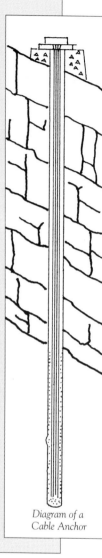

Diagram of a Cable Anchor

Steel caps protect the cable anchors below.

Moving drilling and other construction equipment about the face of the slide called for some ingenuity. Steel ropes, running through pulleys fixed into the rock at the top of the slide, were used to winch the drilling rigs about the face. Only one rig was lost when a pulley failed and the rig, luckily without its operator, crashed to the road below.

Drilling rig on the rock face.

Sheoak Falls make an almost vertical drop of 15m from a series of smaller cascades into a deep pool below. The dramatic effect is enhanced by the contrast between the heavily-wooded, dark green hillside sloping down to the falls and a grassy spur and banks downstream, dotted with graceful sheoaks.

An excellent vantage point for photographs occurs at the junction of the main track and a side track leading back down to the Sheoak Falls.

Immediately adjacent to the river, sheoaks, blue gums and blackwood wattles form the canopy, with blanket-leaf, prickly mosses and Australian clematis being the intermediate layer. Ground vegetation consists mainly of various water-ferns.

On the drier slopes, messmate stringybark dominates the forest with an understorey of silky daisy bush, common heath, bush peas and prickly mosses – all providing a colourful display in spring.

Cumberland River There is a small ocean beach at the mouth of the Cumberland River situated 6km southwest of Lorne, with an interesting cave west of the river mouth. Follow the western bank of the river to the beach and climb over a rock platform until a rock-strewn beach is visible (about 200m). Climb down the rock shelf and immediately on your right is the mouth of **Cumberland Cave** heading back into the cliff. The narrow entrance opens into a huge chamber where there is flow stone and other passages leading deeper into the hill. Don't forget to take a torch.

Cumberland River Camping Reserve Tucked at the mouth of the Cumberland River, protected by cliffs to the east and a cyprus hedge from the coast, with lawns running to the rivers edge creates a beautiful setting for a camping ground. Unfortunately the reserve is closed for camping immediately after the Queens Birthday weekend in June until the September school holidays.

Looking south across Cumberland Gorge towards the ocean.

Picnic tables and car parking are provided at the entrance to the camping reserve.

Cumberland River Cascades Walk

Distance: 3.5km each way *Time:* 2 hours *Grade:* easy

The towering craggy cliffs along the Cumberland River make it one of the most spectacular streams along the Otway coastline.

The walking track is signposted from the northern end of the camping reserve. Although easily followed initially, the track is generally rough and rock-hopping is required for a number of sections. In all, three river crossings must be made on the way to the cascades, stepping stones are in place where necessary. Framed by rocky cliffs bordering the narrow river valley, the Cumberland River Cascades have their own individual charm.

It is possible to explore upstream of the cascades, but the track becomes less distinct and you have to be prepared for a lot of rock-hopping and climbing over massive log jams. The river environment is beautiful with deep rock pools linked with rapids, overhung by massive gums and tree-ferns.

Look out for white-faced herons and spur-winged plovers along the river - birds not likely to be seen along forested walks elsewhere in the Otway Ranges. Just a word of warning–do not attempt this walk when the river is at a high level.

Carbonate nodules imbedded in sandstone

Mt Defiance Lookout This walled wayside stop provides breathtaking views east towards Lorne. This scene is best captured in the early morning light. The Memorial Wall and plaques commemorate the services of the Sailors and Soldiers in the Great War 1914-1919 and was officially opened by Governor, Lord Huntingfield in 1935.

Artillery Rocks west of Jamieson River mouth, are less than 50m from the road side. They are clusters of carbonate nodules embedded in sandstone and resemble cannon balls arranged around ancient guns. The oddly-shaped formations cover more than 100m of shoreline. Few of the formations are larger than 2 metres, but the variety is endless. Beneath

Artillery Rocks yield early Climatic information

The cannon-ball-like concretions of carbonate were formed at about the same time as the soft sediments surrounding them were being consolidated. Chemical analysis of the different isotopes of oxygen trapped in the concretions suggest temperatures during the winter darkness 106 million years ago dipped below freezing.

Honeycomb Rocks

The sandstone underlying the cannon-balls has weathered into honeycomb formations. Honeycomb weathering develops as the sea spray coats the sandstone, leaving behind salt, which crystallizes. As the crystals grow, they wedge against the sand grains, eventually separating them. This forms small holes, which with time become larger and larger.

WALK TIMES **Blanket Leaf to:**
Cora Lynn Cascades 90 mins
Cora Lynn Carpark 3 hours
Phantom Falls 3 hours 30 mins

WALK TIMES **Sheoak Picnic Area to:**
Sheoak Falls 50 mins
Castle Rock 1 hour
Lower Kalimna Falls 1 hour
Upper Kalimna Falls 90 mins
Won Wondah Falls 25 mins
Henderson Falls 40 mins
Phantom Falls 70 mins

KEY
— Main Road
— Minor Road
— Tracks (Closed to Vehicles)
---- Walking Tracks
Park Area

'The Lonely Grave' east of Wye River

AT A GLANCE
WYE RIVER
Distance:
154 km from Melbourne

Accommodation:
1 Hotel/Motel
2 Caravan Parks
2 Bed & Breakfast

KENNETT RIVER
Distance:
159 km from Melbourne

Accommodation:
1 Caravan Park

Grey River Picnic Area

the rocks is a honeycomb platform of weathered sandstone, equally interesting. The site has some of the best developed nodules in the world and is well worth seeing. The concretions also occur at the base of the Upper Kalimna Falls, near Lorne and many other places along the shore platform.

The Lonely Grave & Godfrey Shipwreck (800m west of Artillery Rocks). Just east of Wye River, on the southern side of the road is an historic shipwreck grave. The barque, *W R Godfrey*, built in Greenock, Scotland in 1861, was wrecked near this spot on 8 March 1891. Although there was no immediate loss of life, five men were killed during salvage operations. One of these was a seaman named Godfrey.

Captain Gortley and Seaman Godfrey were buried ashore on high ground. The graves were discovered with a badly weathered marker and inscription, by workers building the Great Ocean Road in the late 1920s. They made the road over the top. In 1930 the present gravestone was erected as a lasting memorial.

It is a coincidence that a pioneer family who farmed nearby was also named Godfrey.

Wreckage from the *Godfrey* including the ribs and anchor are visible on the beach during very low tides. A second anchor and more wreckage remain underwater beyond the breakers.

Wye and Kennett River are popular surfing and swimming beaches. They are 5km apart, between Lorne and Apollo Bay amongst some spectacular coastline. There are frequent lookouts along this section of the road.

Grey River Scenic Reserve From Kennett River take the signposted Grey River Road which runs behind the Kennett River camping ground. A rough track leads up 500m to the top of the mount, where the views are

outstanding. This track is only recommended for four wheel drive vehicles. Two small picnic grounds with wood barbecues and tables are located a short distance apart next to the road along the ridge line before the road drops down into the Grey River gorge. The beautiful Grey River picnic area stretches upstream from the bridge. There are wood barbecues, picnic tables, toilet and running water. Glow worms can be seen in the river bank.

Grey River Walk
Distance : 1 km return Time:1 hour
Grade: easy-medium
The track follows above the eastern bank of the river and terminates at a viewing platform overlooking the narrow gorge.
The walking track starts amongst a tall stand of blue gums and winds through glades of tree-ferns before climbing the side of the gorge. You can hear the cascades below. Continue through a magnificent mountain ash forest to the veiwing platform where you get a birds eye view upstream.

Scenic Drive from Kennett River
Kennett River–Mt Sabine–Barramunga– Stevenson Falls–Wongarra–Kennett River
Distance: 75km Time: 1 day
Take the **Grey River Road** away from the coast and turn left into the **Mt Sabine-Benwerrin Road** passing the Mt Sabine Fire Tower. Turn right into the **Apollo Bay-Forest Road**, and continue north to **Barramunga,** where the **Upper Gellibrand Road** runs west into Stevenson Falls. From **Stevenson Falls** back track to Mount Sabine and return to Kennett River via **Sunnyside Road** south to Wongarra and back east along the **Great Ocean Road** to Kennett River.

Stop 1 *Grey River Scenic Reserve and Walk.*

Stop 2 *Stevenson Falls* are located at the end of the Upper Gellibrand Road, a well formed gravel road which runs west from the main Apollo Bay-Forrest Road. The falls are one of the most popular in the Otway Ranges and are located up stream of the largest camping ground in the Otways on the banks of the Upper Gellibrand River. A picturesque picnic reserve surrounded by pine plantations is located a short distance south of the camping reserve. It is another 500m across a grassy flat then through a fern glade to the base of the falls.

Stop 3 *Mt Sabine Fire Tower* is also surrounded by a pine plantation which does not obstruct the views north west across the basalt plains to Mt Elephant. Picnic tables, wood barbecues and toilets are provided, but you will need to carry your own water.

Stop 4 *Mt Sabine Falls* - A circular walking track leads into the falls from the Mt Sabine Picnic Area located next to Sunnyside Road. Follow the walking track north to the Mill Site which runs parallel with Sunnyside Road. The only reminder of the milling days are the huge heaps of sawdust. The track then swings around to the south, crossing a small gully before descending into Smythe Creek. The final section of the track to the foot of the falls is extremely steep. From the viewing platform you look up a narrow gorge where the falls drop 100m over a series of terraces into the turbulent pool below. This site is even more spectacular during August when the wattles that cover the cliff faces are in blossom and literally turn the gorge gold.

The return path runs south for a short distance and then swings sharply in an easterly direction. It climbs steeply through a pine plantation and then joins a vehicle track that runs up to a fence line. Cross the fence at the stile provided and follow the track back to the picnic area.

Stop 5 *Carisbrook Saw Mill Site* A gate marks the start of the Mill Walking Track on Henrys Road. Follow the track down through the bush to the mill site where exotic vegetation, huge heaps of sawdust and old machinery mark the site. You can also see the embankments of the network of tramways which radiate out from the mill. Imagine this mill and the other 30 like it nearby generating the noise and sawdust as the huge Otway logs were cut into manageable logs.

Stop 6 *Carisbrook Falls*
Stop 7 *Cape Patton Lookout*

Cape Patton Lookout benched into the cliffs 90m above sea level provides views over undulating grazing country with Apollo Bay in the distance. 500m west along the road a walking track leads down to the beach and heads east along the base of the cliffs to the remains of the *Speculant*, shipwrecked here in 1911.

Ramsden Cave is one of the largest coastal caves in Victoria. There is a track leading to the beach just before a farm house west of Cape Patton Lookout. Once on the beach walk east towards Cape Patton for 600m until the entrance can be seen in the cliff above the wave platform. The cave extends 60m into Cape Patton and is divided into two chambers. A large freshwater pool fed by springs is situated 20m from the entrance and blocks access into the second chamber. The pool is up to 1.5m in depth.

Carisbrook Falls Scenic Reserve

The Carisbrook Falls are located in a dramatic gorge a short distance upstream from the Carisbrook bridge, 3km west of Cape Patton Lookout. The Carisbrook Reserve encloses 58ha of natural bush and is the longest and highest series of rapids, cascades and waterfalls in the Otways. The creek drops over 200m in four major waterfalls within a 500m section before discharging into the sea. A short steep walking track climbs the eastern side of the gorge to a viewing platform where there are excellent views across to the falls.

Skenes Creek

Skenes Creek is a small township opposite a beautiful beach with rolling breakers. The town boasts panoramic views over the Southern Ocean and nearby waterfalls, forest parks, beaches and wonderful scenery.

Just to the east of Apollo Bay is the rugged **Wild Dog Road**, a worthy diversion for anyone seeking spectacular scenery. (*Refer to page 58 for a description of this route from Apollo Bay to Lavers Hill*) To the north is the catchment area and reservoirs that supply water to the towns stretching from Geelong to Warrnambool.

An abandoned sawmill tramway and bogie.

AT A GLANCE
SKENES CREEK
Distance:
176 km from Melbourne
Accommodation:
2 Bed & Breakfast

Recorded in the ancient sands deposited 110 million years ago are ripple marks that show water flowed across this area. Minor small coal layers represent the remains of plant accumulations. Not far from here the footprints of a small carnivorous dinosaur were found.

The Speculant wrecked at Cape Patton in 1911.

MOUNTAINS & SEASCAPES OF THE OTWAYS

APOLLO BAY TO PRINCETOWN

Apollo Bay to Princetown

79 kilometres

Apollo Bay marks the transition of the Great Ocean Road from a coastal route to one that carves its way through the Otway National Park to Lavers Hill and Princetown.

The Otway National Park, proclaimed in 1981 covers 12 750 ha and takes in most of the Cape Otway Peninsula. It includes over 60 kilometres of spectacular coastline and rugged rainforests with secluded fern gullies. Today, through the Otway forest there are picnic reserves like Maits Rest with its Rain Forest Walk and the Elliott River Reserve. These have been developed so you can explore the park's diverse forest vegetation.

Worthwhile diversions along the way include the drive to Point Lewis and Blanket Bay, Cape Otway lighthouse and cemetery, the lakes at Horden Vale and the excellent surfing and fishing beach at Johanna.

Lavers Hill township is often shrouded in mist and straddles cross roads high in the Otways Ranges. Melba Gully is located a short distance to the west. The Great Ocean Road descends steeply down the western flank of the Ranges past Moonlight Head to rejoin the coast at Princetown.

Patterned landscape near Lavers Hill

PREVIOUS PAGES
Hopetoun Falls.

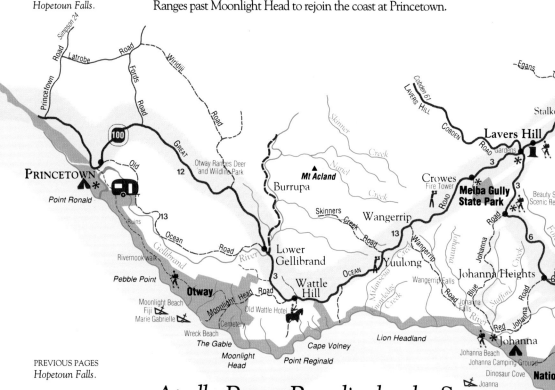

PREVIOUS PAGES
Hopetoun Falls.

Apollo Bay – Paradise by the Sea

AT A GLANCE
APOLLO BAY
Distance:
182 km from Melbourne

Tourist Information:
Apollo Bay
Information Centre
Foreshore
Apollo Bay Vic. 3233
Phone: (03) 5237 6529

Accommodation:
10 Motels
2 Hotels
6 Caravan Parks

Cyprus pines line the Great Ocean Road as you sweep around the sheltered bay and the main street. Lawns dotted with shade trees and picnic facilities run down to the water. The western end of the bay is broken by a break water enclosing jetties which shelter a permanent cray fishing fleet. Fresh fish and crays can be purchased here from the Fishermen's Co-operative.

A public boat ramp provides safe launching facilities for small craft in the wharf area. This is also the starting point for the **Cliff Walk** which runs around the headland to the mouth of the Barham River.

Visitors and locals enjoy a 9-hole golf course, horse riding, tennis, squash, and of course swimming, surfing and fishing.

Apollo Bay is indeed paradise by the sea.

History: In 1840 the Henty Brothers, founders of Portland and Mt Gambier, established a small whaling station. It operated irregularly until 1847 on Point Bunbury, the site of the present golf course.

Timber attracted the first permanent

Wide sweeping beach at Apollo Bay with Otway foothills behind.

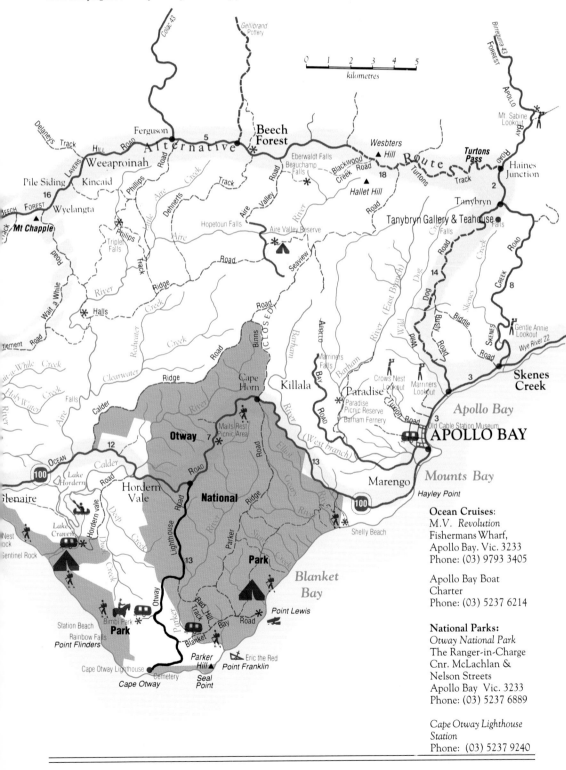

Ocean Cruises:
M.V. *Revolution*
Fishermans Wharf,
Apollo Bay. Vic. 3233
Phone: (03) 9793 3405

Apollo Bay Boat
Charter
Phone: (03) 5237 6214

National Parks:
Otway National Park
The Ranger-in-Charge
Cnr. McLachlan &
Nelson Streets
Apollo Bay Vic. 3233
Phone: (03) 5237 6889

*Cape Otway Lighthouse
Station*
Phone: (03) 5237 9240

Cray-fishing fleet at Apollo Bay

Cray-pots, Apollo Bay

Lush pastures of the Otways

inhabitants to the town in 1850 when it was called Krambuk. In 1846 the bay was named by Captain Loutit after his sloop *Apollo*. He sheltered here from south-westerly gales during a trading trip from Portland. The township was renamed Apollo Bay in 1892.

During the 1850s the importance of timber grew with the demand for sleepers for the new railways servicing the goldfields and piles for wharfs at Melbourne and Geelong. Local timber production was at its peak by 1860 with as many as a 1000 cutters operating. The timber was generally pit-sawn, dragged to the beach and floated out to ships anchored in the harbour. It was a rugged frontier settlement with few comforts.

The township grew again in the 1880s and two hotels were built, a store, a church, school, Mechanics Institute and a library. During the 1860s to 1880s settlers seeking freehold land began the onerous work of clearing the forests for farming. Few prospered and their holdings eventually reverted to the Crown. By the 1890s the Victorian Government realised the value of the forests and withdrew the land not already settled.

In the beginning, access was from the sea, but in 1873 a fortnightly mail service to Birregurra commenced. Coaches negotiated the steep slippery tracks until a gravel road was opened in 1927.

The opening of the Great Ocean Road in 1932 meant thousands of visitors could travel through the cool forests to enjoy the magnificent coastal scenery and sheltered bays with their swimming and surf beaches.

Major Attractions

Old Cable Station Museum is on the Great Ocean Road, 1.6km east of Apollo Bay. This local museum tells the story of early shipping, farming and dairying in the Otways. The Cable Station was the point where the submarine telephone cable entered the ocean to make the first voice link with Tasmania. It was a great day when in 1936 the then Prime Minister of Australia, Joe Lyons performed the opening ceremony.
Open: Daily during summer vacation. Sat, Sun, school and public holidays 2-5pm. Groups by appointment. Admission is charged.

Bass Strait Shell Museum 12 Noel Street, Apollo Bay. A great display of shells collected along the beaches of the west coast, together with Aboriginal implements and photographs of local shipwrecks. The collection covers Australian waters and the Pacific region including some of the worlds rarest shells. Corals and preserved marine life are also displayed.
Open: Daily 9.30 am -8.00 pm. Admission Charged.

Charter Cruises for sightseeing, diving, fishing can be taken from Fishermans Wharf Apollo Bay. A voyage to Port Campbell and the Twelve Apostles can be comfortably made in a day. The M.V. *Revolution* is a 16m cruise boat that can sleep 12 adults and withstand the unpredictable seas along the south west coast. For bookings phone (03) 9793 3405.
Apollo Bay Boat Charter also run criuses; phone (03) 5237 6214 to book.

Scenic Lookouts around Apollo Bay

Apollo Bay is surrounded by places to stop and look out over the forests and spectacular seascapes. **Marriners Lookout** provides excellent views over 30km of coastline from Cape Patton in the east and south west towards Cape Otway. **Crows Nest Lookout** off Tuxion Road is also situated in the ranges just north of Apollo Bay and provides beautiful views over the Wild Dog Valley to the coast. **Gentle Annie Lookout** is situated on a large horse

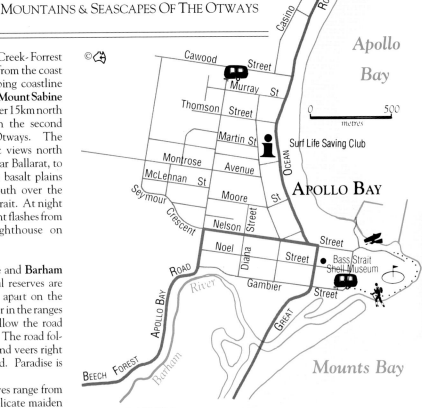

shoe bend on the Skenes Creek-Forrest Road where it rises away from the coast and overlooks the sweeping coastline south west to Apollo Bay. **Mount Sabine Lookout** is situated another 15km north on the Forrest Road on the second highest point in the Otways. The lookout gives panoramic views north east to Mt Buninyong near Ballarat, to Mount Elephant on the basalt plains north of Colac and south over the coastal scenery to Bass Strait. At night it is possible to see the faint flashes from the Point Wickham lighthouse on King Island.

Paradise Picnic Reserve and **Barham Fernery** These beautiful reserves are located a short distance apart on the banks of the Barham River in the ranges behind Apollo Bay. Follow the road signs to Paradise Valley. The road follows the Barham River and veers right into Barham Valley Road. Paradise is 11kms from Apollo Bay.

The ferns in the reserves range from the giant tree ferns to delicate maiden hairs which lap the rivers edge. Massive stands of eucalypt and beech tower overhead to make this a great place to picnic and explore. Some of the trees in the car-park at Paradise Reserve tower over 70m into the air.

Marriners Falls From Paradise the Barham Valley Road continues for another 5km to terminate at a small parking area at 'Willow Bryn'. Marriners Falls can be reached by following the north side of the stream around the back of private property, then continuing upstream for about 1km until Falls Creek enters on your left. Follow Falls Creek upstream into a narrow gorge where magnificent tree ferns, lichens and mosses cling to the sheer rock faces. An unusual feature of Marriners Falls are the massive mountain ash logs stripped of their branches by flood waters and speared into the creek bed at the base of the falls. They look like masts of sailing ships lodged against the cliff faces and give some indication of the power generated during floods.

Marriners Falls

OTWAY RANGES

The steep gradient of the coastal slopes, with their rich volcanic soils have combined with rain-bearing squalls to produce forests filled with ferns, shrubs and tall eucalypts. The area is also cut by many fast-flowing streams, with spectacular waterfalls, cascades and rapids.

The ranges were named by Lieutenant James Grant, commander of HMS *Lady Nelson* in 1800 after his friend, Captain Albany Otway of the Royal Navy. In 1852 the first timber was shipped from the Apollo Bay mill to Melbourne for use as sleepers on the Melbourne-Geelong and Melbourne-Bendigo railway lines.

South of the main Otways ridge the principal tree types are messmate stringybark, blue gum, mountain grey gum and manna gum. At higher altitudes there are magnificent stands of mountain ash, blackwood and myrtle beech. North of the main ridge the forests are drier and the trees not as tall.

A little gold was found along the spurs and some coal discovered near Apollo Bay.

Settlers began to take up land in the Otways and clear the forest in the 1880s. Transport was a major problem, so a narrow-gauge railway was built from Colac to Beech Forest in 1902 and extended to Crowes in 1911.

Sawmills were established in the forest and timber tramways were used for the hauling of the timber to the mills. At the peak of the sawmilling there were 240km of tramways throughout the Otways. Many of these old tramways are now used as walking tracks and the old mill sites are distinguished by their mounds of saw dust and abandoned machinery.

Bird watching
The Otways are among the wettest areas of Victoria, and are swept regularly by moisture-laden mists and rains from the Southern Ocean. Over 150 species of birds, not including seabirds, have been recorded. Birds sighted are Ground Parrot, Crimson Rosella, White-throated Nightjar, Forest Raven (a Tasmanian species), Silvereye, various Honeyeaters, Flame Robins, Tree Martins, Grey and Rufous Fantails, Grey Goshawk, King Parrot, Gang-gangs, Yellow-tailed Black Cockatoos as well as the ground birds such as Ground-thrush, Olive Whistlers and Satin Bowerbirds.

Animals and birds absent from the Otways
No Common Wombats, no Lyrebirds and no Eastern Whipbirds.

Otway National Park

AT A GLANCE
Otway National Park
The Ranger-in-Charge
Cnr. McLachlan &
Nelson Streets
Apollo Bay Vic. 3233
Phone: (03) 5237 6889

Mountain Ash (*Eucalyptus regnans*) is the world's largest flowering plant and one of the world's tallest trees, second only to the redwoods of California. The average height of mature stands of Mountain Ash range from 50-80m, with some specimens reaching to 115m. In Victoria it is found in the protected water catchments in the mountains to the east and in restricted areas in the Otway Ranges. It thrives in the cool to mild summers and cold wet winters where the rainfall ranges from 750-1500 mm per year.

The trunk is long and straight and the crown open and relatively small. The tree is easily recognised by it's rough and fibrous bark at the base which changes into a smooth white or greenish-grey colour above 15m. It sheds in long ribbons, hanging from branches. The wood is straight grained, moderately strong and easily split and worked. It has been used extensively in the building industry.

The Otway National Park covers a large tract of country between Apollo Bay and Hordern Vale, extending to the tip of Cape Otway. The park embraces several types of terrain, from exposed dunes to sheltered mountain gullies, and so supports a variety of vegetation and wildlife.

Some rarely seen birds are found in this park, including the king parrot, powerful owl and the satin bower bird.

There are many minor tracks that can be explored by car, while walkers will find a variety of coastal and mountain walks. Camping areas are situated at Blanket Bay, Aire River and Johanna.

Elliott River and **Shelly Beach** The turnoff is to the south, off the Great Ocean Road just west of Marengo. The Elliott River Picnic Reserve has toilets for the disabled, wood barbecues, water and picnic tables. It is only 500m from Shelly Beach.

Elliott River Walk
Distance: 4km *Time:* 2 hours
Grade: quite difficult
Follow the track downhill from the Elliott River Picnic Area car-park to the mouth of the river. Rock hop upstream for about 200m where there are a set of small cascades. Explore the rugged coastline and then continue via a track along the ridge just to the west of the Elliott River. Follow this track to the Elliott Road and complete the loop back to the car-park. The walk passes through magnificent stands of blue gum.

Geary River Falls Walk
Distance: 2.5 km *Time:* 1.5 hours
Grade: easy
Walk along the rock platforms following the coast south from the Elliott River estuary for about 1km until you reach the mouth of the Geary River. The water falls are located about 200m upstream. Return along the beach.

Maits Rest Explore the Otway rainforest at Maits Rest between Marengo and Hordern Vale on the upper reaches of the Parker River. The reserve was named after a local forester, Maits Brian who often rested his horse there. The 75ha reserve was created in 1958 to protect the spectacular stand of ancient arctic myrtle beeches which line the deep fern gully. The reserve is a place to cool off on a hot summers day, however it is also spectacular during rain squals. Put on your rain coat and experience this unique walk with water cascading and dripping from every overhang.

Maits Rest Rainforest Board Walk
Distance: 800m *Time:* 45 minutes
Grade: easy
A raised board walk has been constructed through fern gullies and around moss covered roots of giant myrtle beeches to help you to experience this unique rainforest without damaging the delicate understory.

Rainforest Gully has been sheltered from wind and fire, the vegetation has remained undisturbed for hundreds of years. The dominant trees here are

Ancient myrtle beech at Maits Rest

myrtle beech which can live for centuries. Their interlaced leaves form a protective canopy, sheltering the vegetation beneath.

Rainforest species flourish in these moist shaded conditions. Giant tree-ferns spread their fronds upwards toward the filtered light. Look closely at the smaller ground ferns. Their fronds are soft and delicate and would dry easily if exposed to direct sunlight.

Keep an eye out for hidden residents. Rainforests provide homes for many creatures. Ground-dwellers thrive in the damp leaf litter, and along the banks of streams and rivers. Have you noticed the 'mud chimneys' by the creek?. They belong to the Land Yabby, a 'compost feeder' which lives on rotting organic matter in the mud. Look out also for the rare Otway Black Snail, a carnivorous species which feeds on worms and other soft-bodied animals.

Not all rainforest plants need to grow on the ground. Beneath the canopy where it is moist and cool small ferns, mosses and lichens have anchored themselves to trunks and branches as epiphytes. Epiphytes depend on their host plant for physical support, but gain their food from dead leaves and other rotting plant matter.

Take a few moments during the walk to enjoy the sounds of the rainforest -water trickling below, wind rustling in the canopy and birds calling.

CAPE OTWAY

'I had seldom seen a more fearful section of coastline', said explorer Matthew Flinders when first rounding Cape Otway. Some 80 shipwrecks and many hundreds of lives later, this beautiful but treacherous 130km stretch of coast between Cape Otway and Port Fairy earned the official title: 'Shipwreck Coast'.

Cape Otway Lighthouse The lighthouse is 21m high and built of sandstone on a cliff 100m above sea level. Because of its inaccessibility the lighthouse keepers received all supplies by sea until 1937. It was just 54 years ago that the Cape Otway Lighthouse Road was finally made.

In 1859 the Victorian Posts and Telegraph Department constructed a telegraph line linking Cape Otway with Geelong and Melbourne. A more ambitious project was the laying of a submarine cable via King Island to Tasmania. This only operated for six months before failing. A cable station was then constructed at the terminus of the cable at Parkers Cove. The partly demolished **Telegraph Station and Signals Residence** still stand near the lighthouse and are a reminder of the first attempt to link Tasmania with the mainland.

The entire project was not a failure however. The telegraph link with Melbourne carried messages from ships making their first landfall since leaving Europe or America. For those on board, Cape Otway was the first dry land sighted since leaving the Cape of Good Hope

Cape Otway lighthouse

Bird watching
Coastal seabirds and Fairy Prion, White-capped Albatross, Green Rosella, and Eastern Spinebill.

Fishing
Point Franklin area and small sheltered beaches. Snapper during late summer, salmon, flathead and sharks.

Experience the Otway National Park on horseback.

• THE NEED FOR A LIGHTHOUSE •

Sailors of the 18th Century soon learned to respect 'the roaring forties' of the southern hemisphere and the huge seas these westerly winds whipped up. Ships could be swamped by following waves, or sunk by icebergs. The icebergs ranged in size from small chunks to floating islands some 120km in length, that drifted north from Antarctica across the Australian sea route. For more than 80 years all ships which sailed from Britian and Europe to Australia had to sail those waters. They came via the Cape of Good Hope and returned round Cape Horn. For over 19000km of that voyage they were subject to the 'roaring forties'.

The route from the Cape of Good Hope to Sydney followed roughly 40 degrees south latitude, round the south of Tasmania and northwards along the east coast to Sydney.

Shortly after its discovery in 1798 Bass Strait was recommended as the shorter, faster route to Sydney. Entering Bass Strait from the west, or 'Threading-the-eye-of-the-needle' required great skill using the navigation equipment of the day. As well, the storms, the fog and the demands of shipping companies for faster times made the voyages very dangerous. For many ships, the first sight of land since leaving Liverpool was Cape Otway and at the same time was their last. Surprisingly, not many convict transport ships were wrecked in Bass Strait, possibly because they were cautious and travelled slowly.

In 1841, Sir John Franklin, Governor of Van Diemen's Land (Tasmania), urged the New South Wales government to erect lighthouses in Bass Strait. King Island was the first preference. Cape Otway was the site finally chosen as navigators preferred to cling to the Otway coast rather than search for low lying King Island.

The pressure for a lighthouse was increased after the tragedy of the *Cataraqui*. It was an emigrant ship bound from Liverpool to Melbourne with 370 passengers and 38 crew on board. It was wrecked on King Island on the 4 August 1845, with only nine people reaching the shore. The wreck became a scandal when bodies were washed ashore and the government called tenders to bury the victims. Pits were dug on King Island and the bodies disposed of in mass graves.

It was left to Port Phillip District Superintendent C.J. LaTrobe to organise a survey of the route from Colac, but the forests and mountains of the Otways proved a formidable barrier. Twice in 1845 he led parties into the forests and twice turned back with men and horses exhausted by the steepness of the country and denseness of the forests. A party led by a Mr Allan marked 'a tolerable road' to within about 8km from the coast, but it was unable to complete the task. In the winter of 1846, a settler, William Roadknight, was able to push the road through to the Cape. The 'tolerable road' followed razorbacks above the Barwon River, then in the distance of approximately 25km it dropped over 1800m from Mt Sabine to, the now, Apollo Bay. From there it followed the shore line, then parralleled the coast another 25km to the Cape.

Construction of the lighthouse was begun by a private contractor in 1846, taken over by the government in 1847, and completed in August 1848. The lantern was constructed by Wilkins of London and had to be landed through surf before being installed in the lighthouse. It had 21 parabolic reflectors, each with its own wick burning sperm whale oil. These were rotated by clockwork; gave a single flash lasting three seconds every 53 seconds; which threw a beam some 22km.

The Cape Wickham light on the northern tip of King Island was constructed in 1861, with a range of 24km, on a 48m tower 85m above sea level.

News of the first gold strikes reached London in 1851, and hopeful goldseekers booked passages for Australia. In 1852, 86 000 people set sail from British ports.

Ship owners needed quicker routes to Australia. An Englishman, John Towson, a watch maker developed accurate, lower-cost chronometers which meant navigators could check their longitude at sea. Towson

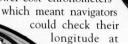

C. J. LaTrobe

also showed that the shortest distance at sea was the arc of a great circle. Winds along this great circle route were also stronger. In fact a ship that curved south on the new route could save over 1600km. With these new instruments some ventured 1000km south of the old sea lanes, dodging the icebergs and riding the mountainous seas of the 'roaring fifties'. They set record times on the run to Melbourne.

Cape Otway Lighthouse

some 11000kms away. Flag signals were made and received from ships passing Cape Otway which took only four minutes to wire to Melbourne. **The Lighthouse Station** is adjacent to the park. The anchor

Telegraph Station and Signals Residence Cape Otway

from *Eric the Red* wrecked in 1880 on the Otway Reef is mounted by the flag pole in the station grounds. Guided tours of the lighthouse and grounds take 1 hour and run daily. Accommodation is available in the historic sandstone keepers house. All enquiries *Phone*: (03) 5237 9240

Protected in the dunes 1km north of the lighthouse is the small **Cape Otway Cemetery** containing the bodies of people who drowned in the many shipwrecks in the area. Also buried there are children from the keepers' families who didn't survive the hardships during the early years.

Bimbi Park trail Rides and Caravan Park is right beside the Otway National Park off Lighthouse Road. Bimbi Park is a 72ha cattle stud specialising in trail rides conducted by local horseman Cyril Marriner. Trails explore the Cape Otway peninsula visiting the lighthouse, farmlands and the remote beaches in the area. Twice a year, in December and early March Cyril conducts an 8 day 'ride of the year' taking in the Cape Otway peninsula from Apollo Bay to the Loch Ard Gorge. *Contact*: Cyril or Pat, *Phone*: (03) 5237 9246

Aire River - Lighthouse Walk
Distance: 11km return *Time*: 5 hours-one way via Station Beach or cliff tops, track goes past Rainbow Falls.

Rainbow Falls Walk
Distance: 6km return *Time*: 3 hours *Grade*: medium difficulty. Springwater flows from a pool situated high on an escarpment near Point Flinders and spills over a cliff to the ocean below, creating the Rainbow Falls. Over the centuries calcium carbonate has deposited on the cliff face and green algae is streaked across the face. When caught by the afternoon sun a beautiful play of colours can be seen.

Access to Rainbow Falls is through privately owned Bimbi Park. Let the Marriners know that you intend walking to the falls. Follow the Bimbi Park boundary fence west for 1km to a gate.

Go through the gate and continue west along the southern side of the fence for another 500m before the track heads south west through low coastal scrub to Station Beach. Before reaching the beach you will see horse yards located near a spring. Continue a short distance along the track before climbing down a small cliff which is the southern end of Station Beach. Scramble south over rock platforms to a small sandy cove where Rainbow Falls can be seen ahead. Retrace your route back to Bimbi Park.

Blanket Bay is accessible via the Great Ocean Road, Lighthouse Road and Blanket Bay Road and is a popular bush camping, walking, fishing and swimming destination in the park. Blanket Bay was the landing station for supplies to the Cape Otway Lighthouse before the road was constructed in 1937. Three seamen drowned here while unloading stores from the supply vessel *Lady Loch* in rough seas in 1896. A memorial to the sailors can be seen in the Cape Otway Cemetery. Ruins of the storage sheds are still visible. At low tide an offshore reef creates a large lagoon which makes a safe swimming beach for children and protected water for canoeing.

The camping and picnic area have toilets for the disabled, wood barbecues, information boards, however fresh water is not available and should be carried. During the summer months it is advisable to book a camping site at the Rangers Office at Apollo Bay.

Blanket Bay - Telegraph Walk
Distance: 6km *Time*: 3 hours
Grade: medium difficulty
The Telegraph Track is 40m north-east of the Blanket Bay Creek (just before you come to the old chimney you will see some timber steps). Follow the track as it climbs steeply up the hill through a very diverse range of coastal flora. At the top of the walking trail is an old four wheel drive track. Follow this through to the Blanket Bay track then turn left and continue for 2km until a cleared fire-break line is seen on your left. Follow this fire-break line back until you overlook the Blanket Bay camping ground. A foot track then runs down to the beach.

Red Hill Track
Distance: 10km *Time*: 5 hours
Grade: easy
The Red Hill walk takes you through some beautiful stands of blue gum which give the appearance of having been planted in regular avenues. The stretch of track cut through heathland in the Parker River Valley is especially beautiful when the heath is in flower during July.

Leave your car at the junction of the Red Hill track and the Blanket Bay Road. Follow the Red Hill track in a

Fresh-water spring near Rainbow Falls

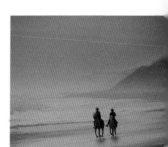

Horse riding along Station Beach

Mouth of the Parker River

Red Hill Track is typical of those in the National Park.

AT A GLANCE
HORDEN VALE-
GLENAIRE
Accommodation:
2 Holiday Flats/ Cabins

JOHANNA
Accommodation:
5 Holiday Flats/Cabins

Looking east over Hordenvale from Glenaire.

Johanna Beach

northerly direction through heath, swampy gullies, messmate and avenues of blue gum until it meets Parker Road. Turn in a south easterly direction back to the junction of Blanket Bay Road. At this point a new walking track has been established across heathlands in a southerly direction just above the Parker River. This track emerges on the southern end of Red Hill Track, turn right to finish the walk back to the Red Hill car-park.

Hordern Vale–Glenaire

Leaving the forests of the Otway National Park the road drops down and skirts a fertile plain formed by the Calder and Aire Rivers. Dairy farms form a patchwork along the valley. Hordern Vale Road which runs towards the coast intersects the Great Ocean Road east of the Calder River bridge and provides access to Lakes Costin and Craven, and the mouth of the Aire River where there is excellent bird watching, camping and picnic facilities and surf fishing on open sandy beaches. Sand Road runs west, parallel with the coast, and rejoins the Great Ocean Road at Hordern Vale.

Escarpment Walk

Distance: 4km   *Time*: 2 hrs
Grade: medium difficulty.
Start the walk at the east side of the bridge at the Aire River camping ground. Follow the sandy 4WD track towards the coast for 200m. Take the left branch of the track and 50m further on turn left and continue up the hill for 500m. At the top, turn right and head west for 1km along the escarpment to find the spectacular views along the coast in both directions. Return via the same route.

JOHANNA

Johanna is a small farming settlement sandwiched between the coast and the Otway Ranges which rise steeply north to Lavers Hill. **Red Johanna Road** cuts through red coloured sand-hills (hence the name) and runs due south for 4.5km past local tennis courts, and over a small bridge to enter the Otway National Park and the Johanna Beach car-park.

A short walk over the dunes opens onto a spectacular surf beach. The beach is not recommended for swimming because of the strong rips when large surf is running. Johanna is one of Victoria's best-known surf beaches however, and is a popular surf-fishing spot. Toilets and bush camping facilities are located east of the car-park.

Johanna Beach Walk *Distance*: 8km return *Time*: 3 hrs *Grade*: easy
Leave your car at the Johanna Beach car-park and take a walk over the dunes to enjoy the bracing air and magnificent seascapes. This stroll takes you southeast along a beautiful flat sandy beach,

crossing the mouths of the Johanna River and Brown Creek. The last 500m is along a rock platform to Rotten Point. Be prepared to get your feet wet when crossing the streams. Rotten Point is located on the west side of Dinosaur Cove. Retrace your steps back along the beach to the car-park.

Sutherlands Beach Circuit Walk
Distance: 4km return   *Time*: 2 hours
Grade: medium difficulty
Start walking on the Johanna surf beach and head in a north westerly direction along the clear sandy beach under high cliffs. Approximately 1km along the coast around Slippery Point is a small cave. The section between Slippery Point and Sutherlands Beach can only be tackled at low tide. Sutherlands Beach is in a small cove where Deep Creek enters the ocean. At the mouth of the creek a very rough goat track heads northeast up on to Hider Track. You can turn back in a southeast direction and follow the jeep track along the ridge between the Johanna River and the sea towards Johanna Beach car-park.

The walk along the ridge offers more superb views along the coastline of the Otway National Park and the Johanna River Valley towards Lavers Hill.

Blue Johanna   Blue Johanna Road is narrow, winding and rises steeply from the coast following a ridge through farmland to rejoin the Great Ocean Road. **Johanna Scenic Reserve** is located on the west side of Blue Johanna road 3km from the coast. It encloses the **Johanna Falls** and the more spectacular **Wangerrip Falls** are located a short distance away on private land. There is no signposting at the reserve, however it can be recognised by the farm house just north of the reserve. The owner has cut a rough track into the Johanna Falls which takes about 10 minutes to walk. Johanna Falls splits into two 50m drops which create a deafening spectacle during periods of high stream flow.

To get to the **Wangerrip Falls** you cross farmland following two fence lines, one west, then south down to the stream which is locally known as the Hider River. Follow the river on the north side through a steep sided fern gully to the base of the falls. Looking up you will see the river plunge over a sheer rock face 80m above. It takes about 20 minutes to reach the falls from the road.

If intending to visit the Wangerrip or the Johanna Falls please let the land owner know your intentions.

The 'Beauty Spot' Scenic Reserve and Walk On the north side of the junction of Blue Johanna Road and the Great Ocean Road is a track sign-posted to the 'Beauty Spot', a picnic area situated 500m off the road, with coastal views.

Beauty Spot Scenic Walk
Distance: 4km return *Time*: 2 hours
Grade: easy
The walk begins at the parking area and follows the old alignment of the original Ocean Road which has riverted to a grassed even graded path winding through overhanging mountain ash, tree ferns and stands of the distinctive native Christmas bush. The Christmas bush blooms in December as the name suggests, when the lilac tinted bell shaped flowers create a spectacular display. In some places you will get excellent views across grassed and forested hills towards the main Otway ridge. The track eventually meets the Great Ocean Road.

LAVERS HILL

Situated high in the Otway Ranges, Lavers Hill is the cross roads of the Great Ocean Road. To the west is Melba Gully and the steep descent past Moonlight Head along the Shipwreck Coast to Warrnambool, to the east the Otway National Park and to the north-east Beech Forest and Turtons Track.

Lavers Hill was first settled in the 1890s, and destroyed by bush fires in 1919. The narrow gauge railway which served the numerous saw mills in the area closed in 1954. Tea houses with their distinctive Australian architecture now provide 'Country Baked Treats' next to open fires overlooking some of Victoria's best mountain seascapes. You can visit the Otway Blackwood Furniture workshop where craftsman can be seen making solid furniture from local Otway timbers.

Mist and cloud often shroud the spectacular views south over the forest canopy to Johanna Beach, but add to the mountain atmosphere that make Lavers Hill a favourite stop-over.

The **Otway Junction Motor Inn** is one of the few along this stretch of The Great Ocean Road.

Blackwood Gully Tea House Walk
A short 10 minute circular walk commences at the Blackwood Gully Tourist Centre and follows the alignment of the Old Ocean Road passing magnificent stands of the huge Otway mountain ash and through a small fern glade.

Gardenside Manor Tearooms and Information Centre overlook beautiful landscaped gardens where you can relax in front of a log fire or stroll through the secluded fern gully.

Scenic Drive from Lavers Hill
Distance: 35km *Time*: Half day
From Lavers Hill drive east to Wyelangta, turn right into Wait-a-While Road and drive south through farms and timbered gullies, lined with monster tree stumps before entering the Otway State Forest. The track narrows

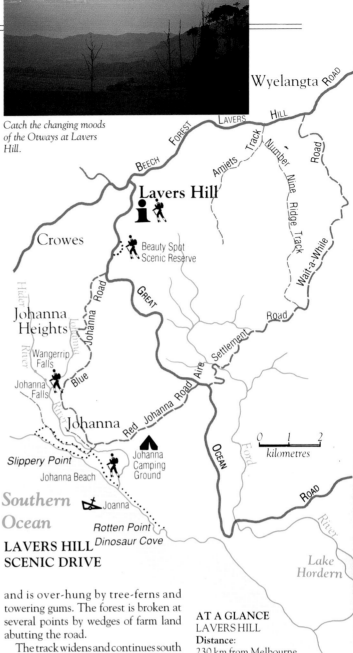
Catch the changing moods of the Otways at Lavers Hill.

LAVERS HILL SCENIC DRIVE

and is over-hung by tree-ferns and towering gums. The forest is broken at several points by wedges of farm land abutting the road.

The track widens and continues south until you leave the forest and pass close to farming sheds and yards. This is now Settlement Road which rejoins the Great Ocean Road another 3km south. (Wait-a-While Road is suitable for conventional vehicles but could become sloppy after heavy rain).

Turn right at the Great Ocean Road and drive west for about 300m and turn into Red Johanna Road which winds down to the Johanna surf beach. The beach was named after a brandy laden schooner *Joanna* which was wrecked near the mouth of the Johanna River in 1843 with the loss of one life. Two foolhardy looters were later drowned attempting to salvage cargo.

Allow time to walk either the Johanna Beach or Sutherlands Beach Circuit Walks (refer page 54). After leaving the beach take the Blue Johanna Road north to rejoin the Great Ocean Road. Stop at the Johanna Scenic Reserve to inspect the spectacular waterfalls. Turn left onto the Great Ocean Road for the return trip to Lavers Hill.

AT A GLANCE
LAVERS HILL
Distance:
230 km from Melbourne via The Great Ocean Road
228 km via Turtons Track

Tourist Information: © 🦘
Blackwood Gully Tourist Centre
Great Ocean Road, Lavers Hill
(03) 5237 3290

Gardenside Manor Tearooms
Great Ocean Road, Lavers Hill
(03) 5237 3215

Accommodation:
1 Motel
1 Caravan Park/Cabins
1 Bed & Breakfast

• DINOSAURS OF THE WEST COAST •

106 million years ago, the area along the Great Ocean Road from Eastern View to Moonlight Head was a broad, flat floodplain crisscrossed by enormous meandering streams and dotted with lakes, with the high ground covered by tall, temperate rainforests.

The fossils of the forests now preserved in the sedimentary rocks are like the Norfolk Island and Bunya pines. As well there are unexpected plants like the delicate-leaved Maiden Hair trees. The understory in the ancient forests had a great variety of ferns, including tree ferns, similar to those of the temperate rainforests of the Otways today. On the floodplain along riverbank levees were an assortment of club-mosses (lycopsids) and scouring rushes (sphenopsids). Millions of years ago these dominated the worlds' flora. The world's first flower species are preserved in the sands and muds that were deposited on these vast river plains.

This was a time when Australia, New Zealand, Antarctica, and South America were one great continent. This was also a time when the Australian peninsula of the remnant Gondwana (which had included these continents as well as Africa, India and parts of southeast Asia) was situated further south. Today the Otway region lies at about 39° south

Partial skeleton of a small plant-eating dinosaur from Dinosaur Cove.

Some areas along the Otway Coast yield more fossils of dinosaurs and their associated fauna than others. One such site is **Dinosaur Cove**, currently being excavated by a research group from the Museum of Victoria and Monash University in cooperation with the Parks and Wildlife Service.

Bones, however, have been recovered all along the coast from **Eastern View** to **Moonlight Head** in the grey-green sandstones, claystones and conglomerates that make up the Otway Group. These rocks are what form the often wide shore platforms jutting into the sea, and the massive cliffs into which the Great Ocean Road has been cut.

As you walk along this rocky shore platform that breaks into the sandy beaches at Lorne, Apollo Bay or Marengo keep your eyes down and look for rocks with odd specks or strange looking shapes. Most of what you will see will be the black fragments of plant leaves, stems, bark and even occasional bits of silicified charcoal that demonstrate wildfires swept through the rainforests some 106 million years ago.

The clays bearing feathers in the Strzelecki Ranges of Gippsland are a similar age to the Otway Group in the Otway Ranges. Such fossil remains of birds have never been recovered from the Otways.

latitude, but 106 million years ago it lay between 75° and 85° South Latitude, well within the Antarctic Circle. For three months of the year, it was dark, 24 hours a day. Studies of the different isotopes of oxygen trapped in the cannon-ball-like concretions at Artillery Rocks suggest that temperatures during this winter darkness dropped below freezing.

In this strange environment, lived a number of dinosaurs. They are most unusual in that they lived so close to the South Pole. The dinosaurs are of two types, the chicken-sized to human sized plant-eaters, the hypsilophodonts, and the small to large carnivorous dinosaurs. From the floodplains the fossil remains of fish (including forms closely related to the still living Queensland lungfish), turtles, crocodiles, plesiosaurs, pterosaurs (flying reptiles), lizards and dinosaurs have been found.

Footprint of a small carnivorous dinosaur, found at Knowledge Creek.

The bones of the fossil dinosaurs, turtles and fish of this region are brown in colour. Should you find fossilised bones contact scientists Drs Tom or Pat Rich, Museum of Victoria, Russell St., Melbourne, (03) 669 9959. Removing material from the parent rock requires some skill. It is also possible to find dinosaur footprints –three have been found in the Otway region, one near Knowledge Creek, east of Moonlight Head and two more just to the east of Skenes Creek. Because the fossil backboned animals from this area are only recently known (most having been found in the last 10 years) what you find may be something entirely new to science, and so is worth treating kindly. Many local people have made important finds of new dinosaur species in the Otway and Strzelecki regions, and some have had new forms named after them.

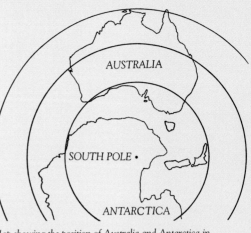

Map showing the position of Australia and Antarctica in relation to the south pole 106 million years ago. The Otway ranges then lay at 75°–85° south latitude, whereas today they are at about 37°.

of food. Many of the trees were probably evergreen and even those that were deciduous would have left a rich leaf litter on the forest floor which could have nourished agile, resilient small dinosaurs. One of the two skeletons of hypsilophodonts found in the Otways (two of the six dinosaur skeletons known from the Australian continent) has another interesting feature. Towards the end if its life this individual suffered from a chronic infection in its lower left leg. Evidence for this is the highly distorted nature of its shin bone. That an individual with such a severe injury lived for some time without falling prey to one of the meat-eating dinosaus suggests that predation of the hypsilophodontids was not intense.

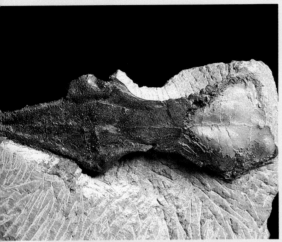

Top of the skull of Leaellynasaura.

The hypsilophodont dinosaurs (*Atlascopcosaurus, Fulgurotherium, Leaellynasaura*) were small plant-eating bird-hipped dinosaurs that were abundant in the ancient Otway region. Bones of juveniles as well as adults have been found. It seems that the Otway region was a nursery for these dinosaurs. Each year they were hatched and grew up in the 24 hour a day sunshine of the summer. What happened to them in the winter is not clear. Some palaeontologists have suggested that they migrated out of the area, but they were so small that it is unlikely that they made such a long trek just to enjoy an hour or so of sunlight each day north of the Antarctic Circle. Perhaps they hibernated, or they may have remained active throughout the long winter night. The eyes of these little dinosaurs were very large as is shown by the large orbital cavities in the skull, and the Australian hypsilophodont *Leaellynasaura* had enormous optic lobes in its brain, where nerve impulses from the eyes were processed. This little dinosaur had good visual acuity - and perhaps it was even warm-blooded.

A dinosaur with these attributes might well have survived a winter in Cretaceous Australia. There would have been plenty

An artist impression, by Peter Schouten, of the chicken-sized dinosaur, Leaellynasaura as it picks its way through the winter undergrowth.

Alternative Route from Apollo Bay to Lavers Hill

Otway rainforest from Turtons Track

Those interested in taking a closer look at the **Otway Ranges Forest** can take an alternative route from Apollo Bay to Lavers Hill, via **Wild Dog Road** and **Turtons Track**. This route passes through Beech Forest and the tiny hamlet of Weeaproinah, which has the dubious honour of being the wettest place in Victoria. A short detour down the Aire Valley Road near Beech Forest takes in **Beauchamp** and **Hopetoun Falls** as well as the **Aire Valley Plantation** where exotic pines, planted in 1929, form a unique forest. **Triplet Falls** are found further west off Phillips Track. This route is not suitable for towing caravans or boats.

Follow the Great Ocean Road east from Apollo Bay towards Skenes Creek for 2.5km and take **Wild Dog Road** north. Wild Dog Road enters a narrow gorge and follows the creek as it begins to wind and climb through steep farm land into the forested ranges above. There are breathtaking views back towards the coast, however the narrow gravel road makes it difficult to pull over and stop, and care should be taken as there are numerous blind corners. The road improves as you enter the forest and the trees virtually grow right to the edge of the bitumen, creating a continuous arch of native vegetation until you reach Tanybryn Junction. Tanybryn Teahouse and Gallery houses an outstanding collection of works from both local and national artists alike. Continue north for a short distance until Turtons Track is sign-posted on your left.

Turtons Track is one of the Otway Ranges most famous forest drives and passes through magnificent forests of mountain ash (*Eucalyptus regnans*) and crosses streams with beautiful fern gullies. The road is mostly gravel, so drive carefully. There are

Fern-gully in the Otway forest

numerous wide curves where parking is provided to enable you to explore the forest. The Aire Valley Road runs south 1.5km east of Beech Forest and provides access to Beauchamp, Hopetoun Falls and Aire Valley Picnic and Camping Reserve.

History of the Aire Valley

The original forests of mountain ash were cleared in the 1890s for agriculture. Lack of adequate transport in those early days meant that much of the valuable timber was ringbarked or burnt. The narrow gauge railway from Colac to Beech Forest was completed in 1902 and provided a means to transport timber products. The timber boom that followed saw many settlers neglect their farms to make better money in the sawmills. At one stage 29 sawmills operated within 20km of Beech Forest. Difficulty in farming the steep and broken terrain, poor access, lack of labour during World War One, and disastrous bushfires in 1919 forced many settlers off their farms. The land reverted back to the Crown or was purchased for a nominal price.

In 1930 the government decided to reafforest the Aire Valley by planting introduced pine varieties. That original plantation now covers the headwaters of the Aire River and at its highest point is 550m above sea level. The terrain varies from moderately undulating to steep and almost precipitous. The valley is also one of the wettest parts of Victoria where the rainfall varies between 1500mm to 2000mm annually.

Beauchamp Falls Road is the first intersection on the right after leaving the Beech Forest-Turtons Track Road. At the car-park there are picnic, barbecue and toilet facilities. The walk down to the falls initially passes through a Douglas fir plantation, then enters lush, native wet sclerophyll eucalypt forest. This forest is dominated by mountain ash and has an understorey of musk daisy bush, satin box, prickly currant-bush, blackwood and tree-ferns. As you proceed towards the floor of the gully, myrtle beech and blackwood take over from mountain ash as the dominant species whilst tree-ferns and ground-ferns dominate the understorey. The return walk takes about one hour.

Hopetoun Falls Back track to the Aire Valley Road and turn left and drive south for 5km where the Hopetoun Falls Road is indicated on your right. It is another 400m to the car-park where you can hear the roar of the water as it pounds over the falls into the Aire River below. A viewing platform is sited near the car-park and a walking track drops steeply down the gully side to the valley floor where it passes through a small glade and tree-ferns to the foot of the falls. The path can be slippery during wet weather. The walk takes about 20 minutes down but allow half an hour for the climb back out.

Aire Valley Picnic and Camping Reserve is only a short drive south on the Aire Valley Road. This is one of the most beautiful picnic and camping areas in the Otways, with its towering

Aire Valley picnic reserve.

Californian redwoods, planted in 1936, forming a backdrop to the Aire River. Some of these trees have reached enormous heights. Facilities include wood barbecues, picnic tables and toilets.

Return along the Aire Valley Road and turn left into **Beech Forest**. Stop at the **Beech Forest Information and Historical Centre** where there is an excellent photographic display depicting early pioneers clearing and milling the massive Otway forests. There are toilet facilities here as well as undercover picnic tables.

Triplet Falls are located west of Beech Forest off Phillips Track. Continue west towards Lavers Hill until Phillips Track is sign-posted on the left running south. Follow this through farmland and young mountain ash until you reach Young Creek. From here there are two sign-posted walking tracks leading to the waterfalls.

The longer walk takes about 20 minutes and winds along Young Creek to a tree-fern-filled valley and a stand of mature myrtle beech. Cascades of water from the three channels of the falls make a spectacular sight.

The other track takes about 10 minutes to walk to the foot of the falls. Old stumps and moss-covered logs on the forest floor are evidence of past logging and regeneration.

Toilets are located in the bush just beyond the junction of Young Creek Road and Phillips Track. Picnic tables and wood barbecues are also provided.

Retrace your steps and turn left into the Lavers Hill - Beech Forest Road and you soon pass through the district of **Weeaproinah** which is the wettest place in Victoria. The weather station here receives more than 2040mm of rain annually. It is only a short drive west to Lavers Hill where you rejoin the Great Ocean Road.

AT A GLANCE

TANYBRYN
Distance:
189 km from Melbourne
Accommodation:
1 Bed & Breakfast

BEECH FOREST
Distance:
207 km from Melbourne

Accommodation:
1 Hotel

Triplet Falls

Melba Gully State Park

'Big Tree' a 300 years old Otway messmate, protected in Melba Gully State Park.

The park is located 1.5km off the Great Ocean Road, 3km west of Lavers Hill. It is also one of the wettest spots in the State with an annual rainfall of over 2000mm. It has vegetation typical of the temperate rainforest which once covered this region. Myrtle beech, blackwood and tree-ferns thrive in the valley, along with the understorey of low ferns and mosses.

One of the oldest inhabitants of the park is the Big Tree, a huge Otway messmate which is over 300 years old. It can be reached by following the main walking track.

Rapids, waterfalls, native birds and animals can also be seen on the walking tracks. The main walk takes about 35 minutes and is well marked.

Glow-Worms The 'night life' is one of the big attractions of the Melba Gully State Park. Rangers often conduct guided tours to see them during holiday periods.

Glow-worms are actually the larvae of a species of small fly, called fungus gnats. They make sticky threads to trap small insects attracted by the glow. These insects are common in dark, damp places and are often found on soil banks with over-hanging ledges in the Melba Gully. They are also widespread in wetter parts of the Otway Ranges.

ANCIENT RAINFORESTS OF THE OTWAYS– TODAY'S LAST SURVIVORS

Many of the magnificent trees that clothe Melba gully are eucalypts, acacias and other familiar Australian trees - but one type, the giant southern beech (*Nothofagus*) is not a common sight in Australia. It once covered vast areas of the continent. It left great amounts of pollen in the 20 million year old muds and clays of northern South Australia and the Northern Territory; and older rocks show *Nothofagus* was even more widespread. During this time Australia lay further south than today, and its climate was cool and wet for the most part-which favoured the growth of great forests. It has been only with Australia's northern drift and its aridification that *Nothofagus* and its wet-loving associates have been severely restricted in geographic distribution. Today it only occurs in patches along the Otway coast and the Lamington National Park, and is also known in such places as the highlands of New Guinea and New Caledonia - and in South America and New Zealand.

The wide distribution of *Nothofagus* forests may be the reason that only marsupials reached the Australian continent during its early history. Such forests support very few vertebrates - and perhaps *Nothofagus* lay thick across the 'bridge' that connected the Australian peninsula of Gondwana with other parts of the supercontinent. It may have blocked the passage of a large variety of fauna -including all or most of the placentals, those mammals that carry their young inside the womb for a long period until the offspring is well developed at birth.

So, as you walk through Melba Gully, you are walking back millions of years in time, into the remnants of a once widespread vegetation that in the distant past hosted the ancestors of our modern marsupials, and parrots , amongst many others.

Vegetation of dinosaur times.

Southern Beech (Nothofagus) *at Melba Gully*

Thousands of glow-worms may live together in colonies creating a delicate light show for the visitor. The glow actually comes from the abdomen and is emitted from tiny tubes which open in the gut of the larvae and are visible through transparent skin at the end of the body.

You should walk quietly when looking for glow-worms, as their light will vanish if they are disturbed by noise or direct torch-light.

During wet weather, you may find glossy black-shelled snails along the tracks. Named *Victaphanta compacta*, this carnivorous species is found only in the Otways.

The **Melba Gully** area was purchased by Mrs Jessie Fry in 1921, and named after Australia's famous opera singer Dame Nellie Melba. Through the 1930s and 1940s it was a popular picnic and lunch stop for tourists, but business came to an end in 1948 when a dimension limit was imposed on buses using Otway roads.

The picnic area is now on the site of old tea-rooms. The large open area was established as a farm; it is being gradually revegetated with indigenous species like mountain ash.

In 1958 the property was purchased, then generously offered to the Victoria Conservation Trust in 1975. It is now managed by the Department of Natural Resources and Environment. Water, picnic tables, fireplaces and toilets are provided. Because of the park's small size, camping is not permitted.

Moonlight Head

Mathew Flinders named Moonlight Head in 1802 when he was charting Bass Strait in the *Investigator*. From his small craft the prominent cliffs were lit up momentarily as moonlight broke through thick cloud during heavy rain squalls.

Moonlight Head is a romantic, windswept location just off the Great Ocean Road, between Lavers Hill and Princetown. The turn off is located on a wide sweeping bend. The old **Wattle Hotel** is located on the south side of the Great Ocean Road at the junction of Moonlight Head Road. The track is suitable for conventional vehicles and winds through thick bush and farming land before emerging onto a coastal tableland covered in low coastal scrub with the ocean before you. The track forks here.

One track leads down a steep incline onto a small plain where the outline of the old Moonlight Head race-course can still be made out. It terminates at a car-park above the cliffs. A walking track leads from here down to **Wreck Beach** where you'll see the anchor of the *Marie Gabrielle* embedded in rocks and the anchor of the *Fiji* another 400m west.

The other track leads to the **Moonlight Head Cemetery** and cliff tops. The cemetery is a short distance from the junction on the left hand side of the track and can be recognised by its rock entrance pavilion and low fence which encloses the overgrown graves. The first burial took place here in 1906 and the last in 1995.

A short distance from the cemetery the track ends in an ill defined car-park where a walking track skirts the cliff tops. The track passes through dense thickets of sheoaks forming an arch overhead. The wind whistling through

Old Wattle Hotel

the sheoaks creates a chilling atmosphere. Only metres away are the highest cliffs on the Victorian coastline. There are several vantage points off the track where you can peer down to the wave platform and boiling surf below.

Moonlight Head Beach, the **Devils Kitchen** and **Pebble Point** are all names associate with gemstone finds. Quartz gravels and pebble drifts are common on the beaches and along the rock platforms around Moonlight Head. They contain rounded pebbles of granite porphyry, mica schist, agate, lydian stone, jasper, pink garnet, tourmaline, topaz and translucent zircon. You can fossick for the stones by strolling along the beaches at low tide with your eyes focused on the pebbles being rolled back and forth with the waves. Some of the agates are very fine with black and white bands with tinges of pink and red. Access to the Devils Kitchen and Pebble Point requires scrambling down

AT A GLANCE
MOONLIGHT HEAD
Seareach Horse-Treks
Contact: Neil Henry and Jenny Venner
Phone: (03) 5237 5214

The view west from the Fiji grave site.

This style of anchor with its easily removable iron stock (cross bar) was the most popular on British ships. The proportions of different sizes of anchors varied as did their weights, and designs became shorter and thicker over the years.

The diameter of the iron used in each link of the anchor chain also varied with the weight of the anchor. Each link was approximately 3 1/2" x 6", with a welded cross member.

Horse riding near Moonlight Head.

landslides and a small cliff and should only be attempted at low tide with the aid of ropes.

The old **Wattle Hotel** set back from the track junction is a relic from the horse-drawn coach days when the hotel was a favourite stopover for guests attending the races at Moonlight Head. It is the only timber building in the area to have survived the 1919 bushfires. At that time the coach road wound past the race-course above Moonlight Head Beach and continued along the rugged cliff tops to **Rivernook Guest House** (ruins still visible) to Princetown where it forded the Gellibrand River.

The reefs off Moonlight head have claimed numerous ships including the French barque *Marie Gabrielle* driven ashore in 1869. The area looked so desolate to the surviving crew that they split up in search of rescue. Three days later the captain, mate and three crewmen reached the Cape Otway lighthouse station, while the second mate and five men stumbled into a settlement on the Aire River at about the same time. Both parties left men awaiting rescue at the wreck.

As fate would have it, the barque *Fiji* was swept ashore a few hundred metres west of the *Marie Gabrielle* in 1891. Bad weather and poor navigational equipment was blamed and despite the rescue efforts of the Port Campbell Rocket Crew and the bravery of a local settler, Arthur Wilkinson, twelve men were drowned.

On the cliff top overlooking the two anchors, the only remains of the *Fiji* are the graves of her drowned sailors. They were buried in coffins fashioned from the ships timbers. A memorial head-stone marks the site.

The Historic Ship Wreck Trail
Moonlight Head is also the starting point for a drive which visits 25 ship-wreck sites between Moonlight Head and Port Fairy. Plaques have been mounted at vantage points close to the wreck sites to help you visualise this dramatic coastline back in the time of sail.

IMPERIAL SIZES OF ANCHORS PER TON WEIGHT OF THE CRAFT.		
Tons	Anchor Length	Chain Diameter
400	9'7"	1 3/8"
500	10'1"	1 1/2"
600	10'7"	1 5/8"
800	11'2"	1 3/4"
1000	11'9"	1 7/8"
1200	12'3"	1 7/8"

MOONLIGHT HEAD

Anchors of the Fiji embedded in the shore platform.

Rivernook Track Walk
Distance: 11km one way *Time*: 4hrs
Grade: medium–difficult
This walk follows the Old Coach Road. It can be started at Moonlight Head, or at the Princetown Recreation Reserve. The track parallels the rugged coastline above the cliffs and passes the ruins of the old Rivernook Guest House. A track runs south from the ruins over the dunes to the surf beach. The scenery along the coastline as well as views up the Gellibrand River Valley are magnificent and the coastal plants and dunes offer much of interest.

Otway Ranges Deer and Wildlife Park
8km east of Princetown.
Eight species of deer can be seen at the park including blackbuck, chital, and wapiti, Canadian Elk and New Zealand, English and Scottish red deer. The park is one of the most developed commercial deer operations in Australia.

Children can hand feed park animals. A variety of Australian birds and animals can also be seen, including kangaroos, emus, wallabies and native birds.

Barbecues and picnic facilities are available. Open every day except Tuesday. Admission is charged, with concessions for families, clubs and groups.

Headstone of the twelve drowned sailors from the Fiji.

Alternative Route from the Gellibrand River to Princetown

The Old Ocean Road leaves the Great Ocean Road immediately after crossing the Gellibrand River bridge and winds along the river flats to rejoin the main road at Princetown. The road passes large wetlands where bird life is abundant, remnants of forest and farming land. The road is narrow and corrugated in places. Look out for dairy herds being moved in the early morning and evening. This is a picturesque alternative to the Great Ocean Road which swings inland over higher, cleared farming land offering views over the Gellibrand River and coastal dunes to the Southern Ocean and Princetown.

Grazing country along the Great Ocean Road.

THE
SHIPWRECK
COAST

PRINCETOWN TO PORT FAIRY

Princetown to Port Fairy
112 kilometres

The Twelve Apostles

'Razorback' east of Loch
Ard Gorge

PREVIOUS PAGES
The Arch

'I had seldom seen a more fearful section of coastline', wrote explorer Matthew Flinders when first rounding Cape Otway. Some 80 shipwrecks and many hundreds of lives later, this beautiful but treacherous 130 kilometre stretch of coast between Moonlight Head and Port Fairy had earned the title 'Shipwreck Coast'. The *Loch Ard*, most famous of all the wrecks is brought to life in the Glenample Homestead Interpretation Centre opposite Gibson Steps.

From Princetown the landscape changes. The Great Ocean Road runs through sand dunes and low coastal heath of the Port Campbell National Park. Sheer limestone cliffs mark the coast. Inland are the low rolling hills broken by occasional patches of remnant vegetation. Glimpses of the awe-inspiring cliff sections can be seen from the road which in places runs only metres from the cliff tops.

The **Twelve Apostles**, **Loch Ard Gorge**, the **Blowhole**, **London Bridge**, the **Arch** and the **Grotto** are spectacular natural coastal features carved from the limestone by the relentless Southern Ocean. The changing moods of the ocean, different light conditions and the violent storms which shoot spray over the 100m cliffs attract thousands of visitors each year.

At Peterborough the Great Ocean Road crosses Curdies Inlet, a broad shallow estuary famous for catches of bay trout and bream. It continues on past the Bay of Martyrs and Bay of Islands and on to Warrnambool where it joins the Princes Highway.

Warrnambool is a fine progressive coastal city that has retained its holiday atmosphere while expanding its manufacturing and service industries. Warrnambool was caught up in the hysteria of a feared Russian invasion in the 1880s and her huge gun emplacements still stand on Flagstaff Hill ready to ward off the enemy. They are near the lighthouse, within the Flagstaff Hill Maritime Village. The village recreates the atmosphere of an early Australian port, incorporating original and recreated buildings, and a collection of historic vessels.

Koroit, north west of Warrnambool, is a graceful town with tree lined streets and a Gothic church without a steeple. Just to the south of the town is Tower Hill, an extinct volcano with island craters.

Leaving Tower Hill the ocean road drops down into a rich volcanic potato growing and dairying area surrounding Killarney.

High cliffs and small kelp covered beaches are characteristic of the Port Campbell National Park

AT A GLANCE
PRINCETOWN
Distance:
261km from Melbourne

Accommodation:
2 Holiday Farms
1 Camping Ground

Walks:
Rivernook Track (ref.
page 63), Point Ronald to
Latrobe Creek Bridge.

Princetown

Situated on the Latrobe Creek, near the mouth of the Gellibrand River, Princetown was named after Prince Alfred. Land sales were held in 1868, but there was no settlement until 1878 when the *Loch Ard* shipping disaster, and the *Schomberg* wreck attracted people to the area. Today Princetown forms the western boundary of the Otway National Park and the eastern boundary of the Port Campbell National Park.

The Princetown floodplain is rich in bird life

At the coast, the Gellibrand River has eroded through ancient sand dunes forming the 90m high cliffs of Point Ronald, while recent sand dunes have built up on the eastern bank to a height of 15m. The flat plain was originally a swamp, and although partly reclaimed it provides a rich source of wildlife and plant species. The surrounding limestone cliffs contain interesting fossils. Years ago, attempts were made to keep the mouth of the river open and free from sand by cutting a tunnel beneath Point Ronald. The entrance to the tunnel is still visible on the western side of the estuary. There is an excellent walking track from Point Ronald west along the clifftops through coastal scrub and sand dunes back to the Latrobe Creek bridge on the Great Ocean Road.

Port Campbell National Park

AT A GLANCE
PORT CAMPBELL
NATIONAL PARK
Tourist Information:
Ranger-In-Charge
Port Campbell National Park
Tregea Street,
Port Campbell Vic 3269
Phone: (03) 5598 6382

Camping:
The National Parks Service camping area has powered and unpowered sites, hot showers and laundry facilities.

Places to Visit:
The Great Ocean Road sweeps past the Twelve Apostles, Loch Ard Gorge and other spectacular features, which are all clearly sign-posted. A walking track also links these features. Take care near cliffs and lookouts, especially when there are high winds.
Glenample Homestead Interpretation Centre.

The park stretches 32 kilometres along the coast from Princetown to Peterborough, and occupies some 1759 hectares. First declared a National Park in 1964 with 708 hectares, it was enlarged to its present size in 1981.

Features such as the stacks, arches, islands, blowholes and rocky outcrops are all to be seen against a backdrop of the Southern Ocean. All the landforms are accessible and signposted from the Great Ocean Road and linked by walking tracks. These natural sculptures include the Twelve Apostles, Loch Ard Gorge, the Blowhole, London Bridge and the Grotto.

The cliffs are composed of Tertiary limestone and marine deposits. The action of the waves working along a line of weakness at the base of the cliffs undercuts them, and when the rock above collapses a sharp vertical cliff is formed.

Blowholes are formed if the rock above a wave created cave collapses. A hole can then extend from water level vertically to the top of the cliff, as in the case of **The Blowhole** .

The **Loch Ard Gorge** is probably a collapsed blowhole, with the gorge widened over time by the weathering of the cliff walls. Arches and stacks may also form offshore from cliff coasts.

London Bridge was a headland with two arches. In January 1990, when the landward arch collapsed, it became an island with one arch. Over time it too will collapse, to form a stack. Stacks may also be formed when harder rock is resistant to erosion. Stacks can vary in size, from small rocky outcrops a few metres above water level as in the **Bay of Islands**, to the imposing giants of the **Twelve Apostles**.

Gibson Steps Last century Hugh Gibson, then part-owner of Glenample Station, cut these steps into the 90m high cliff face. They give access to the beach below, now known as Gibson Beach. He also cut the tunnel through Castle Rock the headland to the west, to give access to the beach near the Twelve Apostles.

The Twelve Apostles

The walk from the steps to Twelve Apostles beach is now closed. The sea is also extremely dangerous for swimming in this area.

Glenample Homestead is outside the National Park, 4km east of the Loch Ard Gorge, north of the Great Ocean Road. Built in 1869 by Hugh Gibson from locally quarried sandstone, Glenample Homestead remains largely unaltered, except for the front verandah addition in 1887. The station was one of the first homesteads on the Port Campbell coast and is an interesting example of Australian primitive archi-

Glenample Station out buildings

tecture. It was also the refuge for the *Loch Ard* survivors.

The homestead is leased by the Department of Natural Resources and Environment and has been restored to its original condition. It is now an interpretation and visitor centre bringing to life the Loch Ard tragedy and showing visitors an original and historic station homestead and outbuildings.
Open: By appointment, contact the Ranger - In - Charge, Port Campbell National Park, Tregea Street, Port Campbell. Admission is charged.

The Twelve Apostles These are stacks of vertically-jointed and flat-bedded limestone, many rising to over 65m above sea-level. Both the stacks and the cliffs are still being eroded by wind and rain and undercut by the ocean, although the wave-cut platform at the base of the stacks and the small beach at the foot of the cliffs is slowing down the erosion process.

The breathtaking sight of the Twelve Apostles standing out to sea, in sparkling sun-shine, wreathed in sea mists or stark against a stormy sea has been an incomparable experience for generations of visitors. The changing moods of the ocean, light, weather and isolation means that each visit is a fresh experience, one to be remembered for a lifetime. It is no wonder that the Twelve Apostles are Victoria's most recognised and photographed natural feature.

Mutton Bird Island The island, at the mouth of the Loch Ard Gorge, is a large stack, 60m from the mainland. It rises 100m above the ocean and includes a giant arch. It is a rookery for some 200 000 Muttonbirds or Short-tailed Shearwaters (*Puffinus tenuirostris*).

On the southeast side of the island, in 20-25m of water lies the wreck of the *Loch Ard,* broken in two and lying on either side of the reef that sunk her in 1878. The wreck was located in 1967.

Stacks are formed as waves curve around a headland and erode it from both sides. First caves are formed, then arches, and then the arches collapse leaving stacks.

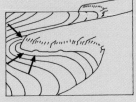

WAVES CURVE AROUND A HEADLAND, ATTACKING FROM BOTH SIDES

CAVES FORM ON BOTH SIDES

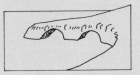

CAVES JOIN TO FORM ARCHES

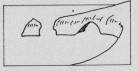

ARCH COLLAPSES TO FORM STACK

• THE *LOCH ARD* TRAGEDY •

Built in Clyde in 1873 the *Loch Ard* was a three masted square-rigged ship of 1693 tons in gross weight, 262 feet 7 inches long and 38 feet wide with a depth of 23 feet. Accommodation on board was very good, with the first class passengers located in the stern under the raised poop deck. The poop, upper deck and deckhouse were constructed of wood and the hull was iron.

At 4am on the 1 June 1878 the haze lifted and about 1.5 km ahead the crew saw high pale cliffs. The man aloft called that he could hear breakers. The *Loch Ard* was doomed. Captain George Gibb sailed from Gravesend, England, bound for Melbourne as master of the Loch Ard. He was only twenty-nine. There were 36 crew and 17 passengers. Gibb had expected to sight Cape Otway, his first land in 15500 km, at 3am on 1 June. At noon the day before, officers took their final sightings. They were inaccurate, probably due to thick haze extending from the coast. Until midnight Gibb continued under full sail, then reduced sail to topsails, jib and spanker. As time passed, without sighting the Cape Otway light, he became concerned and excused himself from the 'final night' celebrations.

When land was eventually sighted, only 1000m away, Gibb hoisted more sail in an attempt to turn the ship around and head back out to sea. The *Loch Ard* swung around, but not far enough to travel through the eye of the wind. Anchors were dropped, but they dragged on the smooth, sandy ocean floor. The *Loch Ard* was now in the line of the breakers with the stern heading towards Mutton Bird Island. The anchors partly held which gave the opportunity for another tack. This may have succeeded but for the reef, which extended from the island. The *Loch Ard* was so close to the island that the yard-arms struck its eastern cliff face each time a wave rolled the ship.

After grinding onto the reef and striking the cliffs, the masts and rigging crashed to the deck and the top deck was torn from the hull. Passengers and crew were either trapped below or thrown into the sea. The *Loch Ard* sank quickly. Only two passengers survived; Eva Carmichael and Tom Pearce.

Sail and rigging of the Loch Ard

Mutton Bird Island

Tom Pearce had clung to an upturned life-boat and Eva Carmichael, a non-swimmer, had clung to a chicken coop and then a spar. The strong sea currents swept both into a gorge and Tom Pearce was able to drag the barely-conscious Eva to a cave in the western wall of the gorge. The gorge was long with a narrow entrance. High walls of some 90m surrounded the water and a small beach.

Tom Pearce, went for help, probably

Eva Carmichael

Tom Pearce

climbing the western side of the headland that juts into the gorge. At the top he was lucky to come across fresh horse tracks which led him to station hands, George Ford and 14 year old William Till, who were mustering cattle for Glenample Station. Eva was rescued and spent some time at Glenample Station recuperating before returning to Ireland. She died in 1934, aged 73. Tom became a sea captain and died, aged 49, in 1909.

The bodies of Mrs Carmichael, her daughter Raby, Mitchell and Jones were washed into the gorge and recovered. Other bodies were seen at the nearby blowhole, but were impossible to recover. The Loch Ard cemetery, sited on the lonely cliff-top over looking the gorge, contains the graves of those recovered from the wreck together with Jane Shields (Eva's companion at Glenample) and some pioneers.

Several days after the Loch Ard sank, a wooden crate was found amongst the debris, which was stacked 3m high across the gorge beach. Inside was a life-size porcelain peacock which was to be exhibited in Melbourne. It is now on exhibition at the Flagstaff Hill Maritime Village at Warrnambool.

The lifesize peacock was created by the Italian modeller Paul Comolera, in the 'majolica' style of chunky, richly-coloured porcelain, for Minton Potteries of Staffordshire, England in the 1870s.

An 1878 Artist's impression of the break up of the Loch Ard

The front cover and two pages of the Salvage Statement of the Loch Ard *reproduced with kind permission of Stuart E. Grant.*

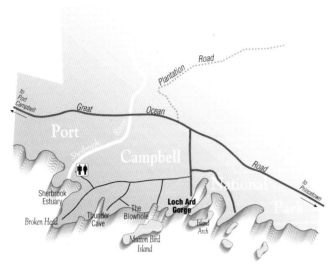

The Carmichael Headstone at the Loch Ard cemetery.

Bird watching
Port Campbell Cliff-tops
The cliff-top heaths contain Rufous Bristlebird, Emu Wren, Tawny-crowned Honeyeater and Blue-winged Parrots. Peregrine Falcons are also in the area.

LOCH ARD GORGE

Loch Ard Gorge At the head of the Loch Ard Gorge, water has percolated through the limestone forming stalactites in the roof of the caves. These caves sheltered the survivors of the *Loch Ard* shipwreck.

The Blowhole At this spectacular blowhole, the sea surges through a 100m long tunnel, up a 17m vertical shaft and erupts from a 40m wide opening.

Other landforms include **Island Arch, Thunder Cave** and **Broken Head.**

The Port Campbell National Park is home to wallabies, bandicoots, and abundant bird life. Over 91 species of birds have been identified, including fairy penguins, pied and sooty oyster-catchers, muttonbirds, hooded dotterels, peregrine falcons, various wrens, quails and parrots. Some are seasonal regulars while others are rare sightings. The coast, estuaries, heath and woodland of the park provide a varied habitat.

There is a small colony of **fairy penguins** near London Bridge. Unfortunately, in the past, foxes have raided the rookery and visitors have accidentally crushed the burrows. To safeguard the breeding colony the area has now been closed to the public.

Fairy Penguin

Loch Ard Gorge

London Bridge after the collaspe of the landward arch.

Mutton Bird Island, near Loch Ard Gorge, is an important nesting place for the **muttonbird** or short-tailed shearwater. These remarkable birds migrate more than 25 000km every year, spending the northern summer in the Bering Sea and returning in September to nest in various colonies in Bass Strait. Until April, when they depart on their long journey north, visitors can watch the birds fly in each evening at dusk to roost. (See page 94 for further information on their breeding and migration.)

PORT CAMPBELL

Port Campbell was named after a whaler, Captain Alexander Campbell, who sheltered in the bay during a storm in the 1840s. Whalers visited the area for some time, before the first permanent settlers arrived in the early 1870s. The town, on the bank of Campbell's Creek, was surveyed and laid out in 1875 by Horace Walker, while the port was established a few years later following salvage operations from the *Loch Ard*.

In 1879-80 the jetty was built and trade started with Warrnambool. Soon after a regular vessel traded with Port Phillip Bay. The postal service commenced in 1874, shops were built and a railway link made to Timboon in 1892. This enabled the town to develop as a holiday resort and three guest-houses opened.

An old cemetery on the northern edge of the town has many old graves including that of Captain Scott and some of his crew, shipwrecked in Newfield Bay, in the barque *Newfield* in 1892. A lookout on the western side of the river offers a scenic panorama of the town and coastline.

The 1 hour self-guided *Port Campbell Discovery Walk* provides an interesting introduction to the park. The track starts at steps at the base of the cliff on

Port Campbell Wharf during a storm

the western side of Port Campbell beach.

Beacon Steps, also near Port Campbell, provides access to the rock shelf at sea level where you can experience the awesome power of the sea. A shipping beacon with basket-work signals once stood on the nearby cliff-top.

The Arch The natural arch formed where sinkholes were created by water percolating through the soft limestone and, together with wave action, eroded the headland. These sinkholes have met in the base of the cliffs of Point Hesse to create an arch.

London Bridge Until 1990 the landform was a fine example of a double natural archway, bordered by a gorge, and backed by a beach, but on 15 January 1990 the landward arch collapsed without warning leaving two people stranded. The huge blocks of the collapsed arch can be seen in the water.

AT A GLANCE
PORT CAMPBELL
Distance:
279 km from Melbourne

Tourist Information:
Port Campbell National Park Interpretation Centre
Tregea Street,
Port Campbell Vic 3269
Phone: (03) 5598 6382

Accommodation:
4 Motels
1 Bed & Breakfast
1 Caravan Park
1 Hotel

Walks:
Port Campbell Discovery Walk.

Boat Charters:
Port Campbell Boat Charters & Schomberg Dive Services
operate two boats out of Port Campbell. Schomberg Dive Services conduct scuba-diving trips to the major shipwrecks in the area, including the *Loch Ard* and *Falls of Halladale*.

Port Campbell Boat Charters take a large cruise boat on regular trips to the Twelve Apostles and Lady Julia Percy Island. Scuba-diving, snorkelling gear and wetsuits are available for hire.
Contact: Phillip Rees or Alister McDonald
Phone: (03) 5598 6499

The wreck of the Newfield.

The Grotto Weathering of the limestone and the collapse of sinkholes have produced a series of hollows linked by a cave which descends to a rock pool. The tranquillity of the area is in marked contrast to the crashing waves a few metres beyond the rocky ledge.

The Moon-gate at the Grotto.

Newfield Bay-Crown of Thorns Rock
The cliffs and ledges of the limestone have been overlain by harder red-brown clays. This harder rock has fallen as blocks to the wave-cut platform below, and over time has been weathered into capping pinnacles, such as the spike-topped Crown of Thorns Rock. Newfield Bay was the site of the wreck of the *Newfield* in 1892.

Timboon
Timboon was settled on the Curdies River in 1877. It became a major timber centre with 18 mills operating. In 1892 a railway linked it with the rest of the state, and the area flourished. An old trestle bridge over the Curdies River is a reminder of the steam train days. The trestle bridge is one of the last surviving structures of its kind in Victoria. Twenty trestles of large diameter bush poles support a timber decking and wharf construction superstructure of spit and sawn timber.
    The area is rich dairy country and

Timboon Farmhouse Cheese, located on the corner of Ford and Fells Road is a family business producing and selling a variety of specialty cheeses. They include Camembert, Brie, triple cream and buetten. Open:10am–4pm daily.

PETERBOROUGH
At the mouth of the Curdies River, Peterborough is a popular holiday town offering a quiet 'get-away-from-it-all' environment all year round. The ocean road by-passes the town centre, but its worth diverting to the lookout at the mouth of the river. From here there are views across Newfield Bay and back over the golf course sandwiched between the sand dunes and the town. A granite cairn near the lookout is in memory of James Irvine who drowned while attempting to cross the river on horse back in 1919. Peterborough is surrounded by small secluded beaches and coves which are great to explore and offer protection from the wind. The Curdies River estuary is also a sheltered safe swimming spot for children and others trying to learn to windsurf.
    The clipper *Schomberg* was wrecked at the mouth of Curdies River in 1855. A plaque on the '**Historic Shipwreck Trail**' located near the river mouth, describes this as well as the *Newfield* and *Young Australian* wrecks.
    Peterborough township was surveyed by Nathan Thornley in 1866. When lots were offered for sale, 40 of the 60 blocks were sold, mainly to speculators. The first house was not built until 1873. There are two boat launching ramps at Peterborough. The ocean ramp runs off the car-park at the mouth of the Curdies River and is used in calm weather to give boat access into Newfield Bay. The Curdies River ramp is north of the bridge past the caravan park and only recommended for small boats with a shallow draught able to negotiate the shallow inlet.

Curdies Inlet is a wide shallow estuary with a single deep channel that winds

Peterborough and Curdies Inlet

its way to the narrows, the point where the river meets the inlet. The 'narrows' and upstream along the Curdies is one of Victoria's best known bream fishing spots.

A favourite excursion from Peterborough is an early morning fishing trip on Curdies Inlet followed by a counter meal at the **Boggy Creek Hotel** at Curdievale. A channel has been cut from the river into the landing jetties at the end of the beer garden to cater for river traffic. The Boggy Creek Pub has a tradition of fine food served in a relaxed country atmosphere. There is also a boat launching ramp at Curdievale providing access to the river for larger craft.

The stretch of the Curdies River upstream of the inlet can be reached by road. Turn right on the outskirts of Peterborough and head northwest for 3km until a gate on your right marks the track which runs down to the river. A sign on the gate indicates the condition of the track which is maintained by a local farmer who even goes to the trouble of mowing the river bank to increase your enjoyment. This is a beautiful stretch of river. Make sure it is not spoiled by leaving rubbish. Bait can also be caught on site. Shrimps and grey back minnows are prolific in the weed along the river bank.

Bay of Islands The bay is a constantly changing picture of rolling breakers parting around irregular islands and rock stacks with their screeching sea birds. The waves finally dissipate their energy on the sheltered beaches at the bottom of sheer limestone cliffs.

Although smaller than the stacks of the Twelve Apostles, the Bay of Islands gives a closer and more intimate view of the landforms.

The Bay of Islands boat ramp must be the longest and steepest in Australia. Its fascinating to watch locals effortlessly drive straight down the narrow ramp that drops to the small beach below. The boat is launched and the vehicle turned for the steep climb out. This ramp is not recommended unless you are very competent in handling your four wheel drive and should only be attempted at low tide.

Bay of Islands Walk
Bay of Island car-park to western headland
Distance: 3km   *Time*: 2 hours return
Grade: medium
The walk takes you through some magnificent coastal scenery. From the car-park follow a four wheel drive track west. At a fork take the path to the left to look over the bay. Retrace your steps and follow the other track to a scrubby gully where there is a safe crossing a little upstream.

Following tracks where possible, con-

Bay of Islands

tinue along the coastline to your left, past a small island and a waterhole. Cross another gully near an old fence line and continue west along the coast until an overgrown track climbs gently to the south. You can look out over the bay from here with Peterborough in the distance. It is a short walk over grassy slopes to the cliff edge. A stunning panorama opens up before you, with the sea lapping the base of the cliff 30m below. Take extreme care in this area, especially if it is windy.

Retrace your steps to the old vehicle track and follow it north until it intersects a track running east-west. The fence line running parallel with the track is the northern boundary of the Bay of Islands Coastal Reserve. Return to the car-park along this track to the right. You will need to cross a steep-sided, thickly timbered gully. Continue along the track keeping two fences on your left. The track eventually veers to the right. Follow it through very thick coast wattle and heath to the Great Ocean Road. A short walk to the right (south) brings you to the gravel road leading to the car-park.

AT A GLANCE
PETERBOROUGH
Distance:
292km from Melbourne

Accommodation:
1 Hotel/Motel
1 Motel
2 Caravan Parks

Walks:
Bay of Islands Walk

Curdies River Access Track

Shipwreck Trail marker at the mouth of the Curdies River.

CAPTAIN JAMES 'BULLY' FORBES, THE *SCHOMBERG* AND SHIPWRECKS

One of the famous clipper ship captains was the notorious James 'Bully' Forbes. Forbes was 18 years old when he first went to sea in 1839. At 31 he was captain of the *Marco Polo,* in which he established a new record, of 5 months 21 days, for the Liverpool to Melbourne round trip. He followed the great circle route. He had no consideration for the passengers or his crew and drove them until they dropped in his quest for faster times. So fast were his trips that he was rewarded with an even faster clipper ship, the *Lightning.* In 1854 he achieved 77 days from England and 64 on the return, a record never beaten by a sailing ship.

At the peak of his career, Forbes took over the *Schomberg*, a huge ship, 2284 tons, 247 feet long, with masts 190 feet and yard arms of 90 feet. It carried 16000 square yards of canvas and could transport 1000 passengers and 130 crew in comfort. Acclaimed as the fastest and most perfect sailing vessel ever built the *Schomberg* left England on her maiden voyage on 6 October 1855 headed for Melbourne. The trip was slow [80 days] due to adverse winds, and the coast of Australia was sighted on Christmas Day. Two days later she was grounded on a sandbank near Peterborough. There were no casualties.

Forbes had been drinking and playing cards below deck at the time. The *Schomberg* broke up on 6 January 1856, but even so it kept on moving. The stern went to the bottom in 10m of water just off Schomberg Reef, but the bow drifted to New Zealand, and landed sometime before 1870, not far from the mouth of Tauperikaka Creek on the South Island, 2 414 kms away.

The Schomberg Diamond, rudder fittings and models of the ship are on display at Flagstaff Hill Maritime Village.

Some of the wrecks of the Shipwreck Coast

Barque: 3 or more masts, square rigged except for aftermast.
Brig: 2 masts with square sails on each mast, and fore and aft sails.
Clipper: 3 or more masts, all square rigged with streamlined hulls, the ultimate in sailing ship construction.
Schooner: 2 or more masts, fore- and aft-rigged.

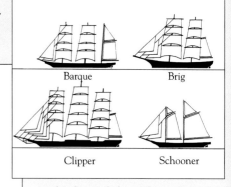

Year	Ship	Type	Location
Pre 1800	Mahogany Ship		Between Port Fairy and Warrnambool
1836	Sarah Ann	Cutter	Port Fairy
1837	Thistle	Schooner	Port Fairy
1838	Children	Barque	Childers Cove
1840	Mary Ann	Barque	Port Fairy
1841	Dusty Miller	Schooner	Port Fairy
1842	Truganini	Schooner	Warrnambool
1844	Elizabeth	Schooner	Port Fairy
1846	Squatter	Schooner	Port Fairy
1849	Minerva	Schooner	off Cape Otway
1850	Enterprise	Schooner	Warrnambool
1852	Lillias	Schooner	Warrnambool
1854	Osprey	Schooner	Lorne
1854	Anna	Brigantine	Apollo Bay
1855	Schomberg	Clipper	Peterborough
1857	S.S. Champion	Ship	off Otway Coast
1859	Admella		Portland
1862	Tubal Cain	Ship	SW of Cape Otway
1864	Fair Tasmanian	Brig	Warrnambool
1866	Ant	Steamer	Bream Creek
1869	Marie Gabriel	Barque	Moonlight Head
1876	Water Lily	Schooner	Port Fairy
1878	Loch Ard	Clipper	Mutton Bird Island
1878	Napier	Paddle steamer	Port Campbell
1880	Eric The Red	Clipper	off Cape Otway
1891	Nowra	Barque	London Bridge Reef
1891	Fiji	Barque	Moonlight Head
1892	Newfield	Barque	Peterborough
1894	Freetrader	Barque	Peterborough
1908	Falls of Halladale	Barque	Peterborough
1911	Speculant	Barquentine	Cape Patton
1921	Nestor	Motor Craft	Warrnambool
1932	Casino	Steamer	Apollo Bay
1940	City of Rayville	Ship	off Cape Otway

Another ship wrecked west of Peterborough was the Falls of Halladale . It was bound for Melbourne from New York in 1908. Sea-mist confused the captain who had all sails set when the Falls of Halladale struck a reef, and ran up onto it. It was totally wrecked, but not before it became a tourist and photographers attraction.

Childers Cove west of Peterborough was the site where the barque, *Children* sank in 1838. It was a coastal trader, on a trip from Launceston to Portland when it was blown off course and struck a reef. Seventeen crew were drowned. The cove has sandy protected beaches. Barbecue and picnic facilities are located next to the car-park over looking the beach.

Sandy Bay to Stanhope Bay Walk
Distance: 4.5km *Time*: 3 hours
Grade: medium
The walk begins on the large sweeping bend as you enter the Childers Cove Reserve and runs east into Dog Trap and Stanhope Bays.

Walk along the sandy four wheel drive track to the beach. Buckley's Creek enters the eastern end of the bay and is best crossed close to the incoming waves. Climb steeply through broken rocks out of the bay for excellent views of the off-shore rock stacks and the distant headlands of Port Fairy and Portland to the west and Buttress Point to the east. Continue east through low coastal vegetation to another track. Follow this to a Y-intersection and take the right fork to Dog Trap Bay. There is access to the beach from this point.

Continue around the clifftops until the track ends. 100m beyond is an extensively-eroded gully which can be skirted by a detour to the left. A short distance away is Stanhope Bay. Access to the beach is possible at low tide via a steep path which is extremely slippery when wet.

The rope 'hand-rail' should not be relied upon and small children will need close supervision. It is hard to imagine that a boatshed once nestled under these towering cliffs.

You can return inland along a minor road through pleasant undulating farmland. At the bitumen road, turn left to return to the starting point.

Ralph Illidge Sanctuary is 32km east of Warrnambool on the Warrnambool-Cobden Road. This is one of the few remnants of natural bushland in the Western District and has been declared a sanctuary. Photographer Ralph Illidge, bequeathed his 40ha property to the State in 1975 and called it 'Bimbimbi' meaning 'place of many birds'. He wanted to preserve the richness of the bird life and the magnificent flora. A further 40ha of adjoining land was purchased in 1986. It is a home for the rare potoroo, the powerful owl, the rufous bristle bird and white goshawk.

Barbecue and picnic facilities are provided. Admission is free, but donations for the maintenance of the sanctuary are appreciated.
Open: Saturday and Sunday 11am-6pm.

'Charmwoods' Nullawarre 35km east of Warrnambool, is a modern rotary dairy open to visitors. *Open*: Daily 4.15pm-5.30pm. Admission is charged.

Allansford is a pleasant country town dominated by three cheese processing factories; the Warrnambool Butter and Cheese factory, Kraft's largest Australian cheese factory and another plant for cutting and packing cheese.
Allansford Cheese World has over a 100 varieties of Australian cheese and 50 varieties of wine on display and for sale, together with honey and cream. The centre offers cheese tasting, licenced restaurant, plus picnic and barbecue areas.
Open: Monday to Fri. 8am-4pm, Sat. 9am-1pm. Extended hours during summer school holidays.

The Potoroo is the smallest Victorian member of the Kangaroo family. It is nocturnal, slightly smaller than a rabbit, and is dark brown and sometimes the tail is white-tipped. They were once widespread and common in south-eastern Australia, but are now restricted to isolated colonies.

A wide range of cheese and wine is for sale at Allansford Cheese World.

Hopkins Falls 13km northeast of Warrnambool. Known as the mini-Niagara, they are a spectacular sight in flood, or in early summer when the annual migration of eels takes place. The tiny elvers can be seen fighting their way upstream over the slippery rocks. Picnic and barbecue facilities are provided.

Alternative route into Warrnambool from the Great Ocean Road
Instead of joining the Princes Highway north of Allansford turn west through the township and left again into Tooram Road which runs south towards the coast.

Hopkins Point Road is signposted and runs between the Hopkins River and the coast, passing Logans Beach whale viewing platform and Fletcher Jones & Staff gardens before joining Raglan Parade in the heart of Warrnambool. The Tourist Information Centre is on your right. Caravan parking is provided.

Childers Cove

Warrnambool

AT A GLANCE
WARRNAMBOOL
Distance:
353km from Melbourne
via the Great Ocean
Road
264km via Princes
Highway

Tourist Information:
*Warrnambool Visitor
Information Centre*
600 Raglan Parade,
Warrnambool Vic 3280
Phone : (03) 5564 7837

Sited on Lady Bay, Warrnambool is a beautiful provincial city that has retained its holiday atmosphere while expanding its manufacturing and service industries. It is also a major stopover for travellers on the Great Ocean Road.

The sounds of creaking sailing vessels, the narrow cobble-stoned paths and the quaint buildings at Flagstaff Hill Maritime Village captures the atmosphere of an early Australian port and acts as an interpretation centre for the Shipwreck Coast.

Between June and October you may also see one of nature's most remarkable creatures, the Southern Right Whale and calfs frolicking in the surf off Logans Beach.

Sheltered near the mouth of the Hopkins River is the beautifully restored 19th Century boat house. Along with its jetties and boats it revives a bygone era.

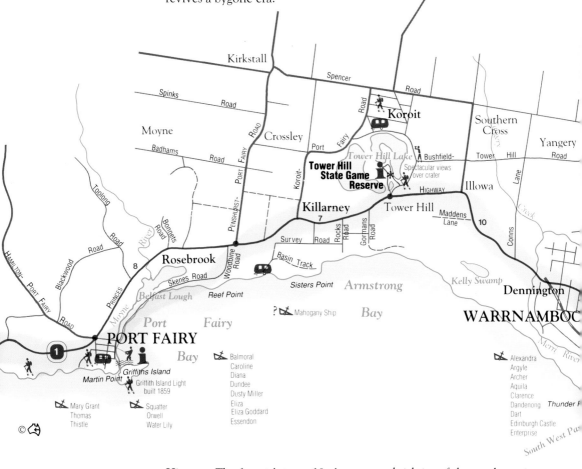

History: The first sightings of Lady Bay, in December 1800, were accredited to Lieutenant James Grant commander of the 60 ton brig, *Lady Nelson*, a vessel specially designed for exploration. In 1802, the French navigator and scientist Captain Nicolas Baudin, in the ships *Géographe* and *Naturaliste*, marked Point Pickering and Tower Hill on his charts, but he did not land.

There is a possibility that Warrnambool's history extends back to 1522 when the mysterious Spanish, Chinese or Portuguese 'Mahogany Ship' was wrecked in the vicinity of Armstrong's Bay, sited between Warrnambool and Port Fairy. The first

reported sighting of the wreck was in 1836 by two shipwrecked sailors who were making their way back to Port Fairy. The wreck disappeared in 1880, presumably under shifting sand dunes. Its rediscovery could rewrite Australia's history. Searches for the 'Mahogany Ship' were made in 1890, 1908-10, 1974-75, 1975-76 and 1981, all without success.

Sealers and whalers sporadically used Lady Bay as a safe anchorage during the early years of the 19th Century until the first permanent settlers arrived in 1839. The village was founded in 1847 and had a rapid development because of its rich agricultural hinterland. The

Hopkins River Boathouse is classified by the National Trust.

Accommodation:
24 Motels
 7 Hotels
12 Holiday Flats/Guest
   Houses
 6 Caravan Parks
10 Bed & Breakfast
 3 Hostels

Attractions:
Flagstaff Hill Maritime Museum, Logans Beach Whale Observation Platform, May Racing Carnival, Fletcher Jones & Staff Gardens, Botanic Gardens, Performing Arts Centre, Warrnambool Art Gallery, Customs House Gallery, History House, Hopkins Falls, Hopkins River Boathouse, Wollaston Bridge, Lake Pertobe and adventure play ground, Warrnambool Aquarium, Thunder Point Coastal Reserve and Allansford Cheese World

municipality was proclaimed in 1855 and town status was reached in 1883. Warrnambool was proclaimed a city in 1918. The name was originally spelt 'Warnimble', the Aboriginal word meaning 'plenty of water'.

Lady Bay

There are six Aboriginal sites registered by the Victoria Archeological Survey near Lady Bay. One 'midden' could date back some 80 000 years which would make it the oldest in Australia. Middens

Hopkins Falls in full flood.

Picnic Spots:
Albert Park Coulstock &
Cramer Streets,
Botanic Gardens Queen
& Cockman Streets,
Hopkins River mouth off
Blue Hole Road,
Cannon Hill off Artillery
Crescent,
Fletcher Jones Gardens
Flaxman Street,
Lake Pertobe Pertobe
Road,
Payne Reserve and *Merri
River* at Dennington.

Walks:
Excellent maps with
notes are available at
the Visitor Information
Centre.

Heritage Trail
Distance: 3km
Time: 1 hour
This trail gives an
introduction to
Warrnambool's early
central area, with its
collection of commercial
buildings from the
Victorian era.

are normally found in sand dunes near
the place where shell-fish were collected
and eaten over many years. They consist of broken shells mixed with charcoal, stone flakes, pebbles and bone
fragments.

Warrnambool's Lady Bay has never
been an ideal port. It is notorious for
unpredictable weather, dangerous reefs
and shallow water. Its entrance cannot
be negotiated in heavy seas and it is
exposed to the south-easterly winds.
But the Port of Warrnambool was of
major importance to the town's growth.
In the 1840s sailing time to Melbourne
was one and half days while the land
route took six weeks by bullock wagon.
In the early days ships' cargo and passengers were unloaded onto lighters and
rowed ashore.

Jetties were constructed to meet the
immediate needs of shipping.
Thornton's Jetty, Tramway Jetty and

the tramway were constructed be-
tween1854 and 1876, and extended
220m into deep water.

In an effort to make the anchorage
safe, plans for the construction of a
breakwater were made in 1859. Work
began in 1880 and completed in 1915.
The siltation of the bay has occurred
since, and low sand dunes now cover
the area where the Tramway Jetty once
stood.

Twenty eight shipwrecks were
documented between 1836 to 1905.
Some are still on the sea floor of Lady
Bay, others are covered by sand dunes.
Historic markers along the foreshore
pinpoint the most significant wrecks.
They include; *Whaleboat* (mouth of
Hopkins River) 1836, *Enterprise* 1850,
Freedom 1853, *Golden Spring* 1863,
Alexandra 1882, *Yarra* 1882, *Edinburgh
Castle* 1888, *Freetrader* 1894 and *La Bella*
1905.

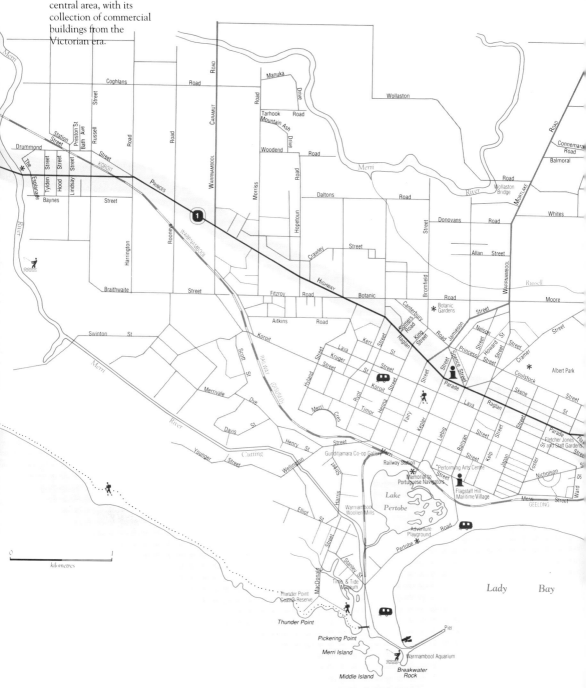

FLAGSTAFF HILL
MARITIME MUSEUM

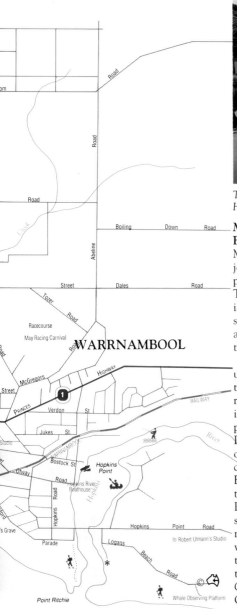

The restored ketch Reginald M *at Flagstaff Hill Maritime Museum.*

Major Attractions
Flagstaff Hill Maritime Museum
Merri Street, is one of Victoria's major tourist attractions developed to preserve Australia's maritime history. The atmosphere of an early Australian port is recreated and historic vessels are preserved. The village is built around the original lighthouse and the 1887 fortifications of Warrnambool.

The story of shipping and the sea unfold as you tour the village. As well there are re-enactments of shoot-outs, robberies and arrests. A prize exhibit is the Loch Ard Peacock, a life size porcelain peacock created by sculptor Paul Comolera and fired by Mintons of England in 1851. The peacock was destined for The Great International Exhibition in Melbourne on board the ill-fated *Loch Ard* wrecked near Port Campbell in 1878. The peacock survived the shipwreck, and after almost 100 years in a private collection, was purchased by Flagstaff Hill Maritime Museum at auction. Guided group tours are available.

Open: 9am–5pm daily excluding Christmas Day

Admission is charged.

Model room Flagstaff Hill

Walks:
Thunder Point-Levy's Point
Distance: 9km
Time: 4 hours
This walk through dune heathland, features coastal scenery, Aboriginal middens and abundant bird life.

Hopkins River Mouth
Distance: 2km
Time: 1 hour return
An attractive walk through marram grass, coast beard-heath and tea-tree along the river estuary and the beach of Lady Bay. The track passes Granny's Grave. The last section of the walk is more difficult at high tide.

Mahogany Ship
Distance: 12km *Time:* 5 hours return
The walk to the site of a recent survey searching for the mysterious Mahogany Ship wreck passes through swamp land teeming with a wide variety of bird life.

Logans Beach
Distance: 9km *Time:* 4 hours return
This is a walk along the sandy beach, famous for the sightings of the Southern Right Whale, to areas of ancient sandstone cliffs.

Fishing
River:
Hopkins River: Bream, estuary perch, Mulloway and Mullet. At certain times Salmon and Trevally.
Merri River: Bream, Mullet and brown trout.
Breakwater and Rocks: Yellow-tail kingfish, tuna and a variety of sharks.
Reef: Snapper, Sweep, Salmon, Pike, Barracouta, and Whiting.
Surf: Salmon, Snapper, Mulloway and Shark.

The Flagstaff Hill Maritime Village Tapestry was designed and woven by local weavers, Gerda Shanley, Beryl Conlan and Judith Stewart. It measures 9.5m by 0.7m.

Logans Beach Located 2km east of the city, Logans Beach is well sign posted. Follow Hopkins Road, turn right just over the bridge onto Blue Hole Road and left onto the Logans Beach Road. Follow it to the lookout. Take a pair of binoculars to get a closer look at the majestic whales.

Warrnambool has once again become the 'Southern Right Whale Nursery' and attracts thousands of visitors to marvel at the survival of the whales once hunted nearly to extinction.

'Warrnambool Grand Annual Steeplechase' Race goers and punters flock to the 'May Racing Carnival' each year. It starts on the Tuesday before the first Thursday in May and builds up to the main events, the 'Warrnambool Grand Annual Steeplechase' and 'Warrnambool Cup' on the Thursday. Warrnambool literally bursts at the seams. Motels feature live bands and other entertainment and a favourite night spot is Burkes Koroit Hotel where music and singing run into the small hours of the morning.

The first steeplechase was held in 1872. Now with international recognition, the particularly gruelling course of 5500m and 33 fences ventures into nearby paddocks and across the road.

Around Lady Bay
Lake Pertobe, sheltered behind the foreshore is a great place for children. A network of lakes and islands linked by bridges and dotted with adventure play equipment has been created by the City Council. During the summer children

Memorial to Portuguese navigators overlooking Lake Pertobe and Lady Bay.

take to the water in mini powerboats, canoes and paddleboats. The children on land can get lost in the maze or try the Tarzan swing and the flying fox.

Warrnambool Aquarium Breakwater Point. The display includes many sea fish species and a large collection of shells. Admission is charged.

Wollaston Bridge

Wollaston Bridge This 19th Century cable suspension bridge was erected across the Merri River in 1890 by Arthur Dudley Dobson (who also built the Warrnambool breakwater). The bridge superstructure is suspended on steel cables taken from the old cable trams of Melbourne, and anchored with square-tapered stone towers. The planking is red gum and yellow box. It has withstood a hundred years of floods, and is classified by the National Trust.

Thunder Point Coastal Reserve is located 2km south-west of Warrnambool, Thunder Point is the inland section of a 80 000 year old sand dune. The sea section has been eroded away and all that is left are island platforms.

Within the 50ha reserve are a number of multiple layered Aboriginal middens. The middens consist of stone flakes, shells, crayfish remains, seeds, charcoal and bone fragments. They are between 3000 and 7000 years old.

The reserve is a great area for sightseeing, relaxing, bird watching and walking. You can line and spear fish all year round. Spear-fishing is prohibited

• WHALES AND THE WEST COAST •

Over the past decade sightings of whales off the Australian coast are becoming more frequent. They include the Southern Blue Whale, Killer Whale, Pilot Whale, Sperm Whale, Minke Whale, Humpback Whale and the Southern Right Whale.

Right whales are large, heavy-bodied animals with thick blubber. It was the combination of the high-yielding oil, from the blubber, and the fine baleen (whale bone) that gave them their name, meaning the 'right' whales to hunt. Southern Right Whales were hunted in the Pacific at the end of the 18th to the early 19th Century. Over 200 000 whales were killed bringing it close to extinction.

There are three main groups of baleen whale which includes the 'Right Whales'. The Southern Right Whale (*Balaena glacialis australis*). The Pygmy Right Whale (*Caperea marginata*) all found in Bass Strait.

Southern Right Whale

This is a stocky whale, with a barrel-shaped body and a very large head about 1/4 of the total body size. The mouth is bowed sharply upward and lined on the upper jaw with about 250 baleen plates (teeth) up to 2.2m long. The baleen is a material similar to our fingernails and is used for straining anything edible when water is expelled past the lips.

The head and mouth region are marked with skin thickenings (bumps) or callosities on the upper and lower jaws and above the eye. The pattern varies from one whale to another so an individual can be identified. The callosities are home to barnacles, parasitic worms and whale lice.

The whale is a slow swimmer, cruising at 3-9 km/hr. It remains on the surface for 5-10 minutes, exhales about 6 times them submerges for 10-20 minutes. The Southern Right Whale breeds once every two years. Calfs are born in winter after a 9-10 month gestation period and are suckled for about 12 months. Females come into shallow water to calf, some times only a short distance behind the breakers. The males remain out to sea. They do not feed during the mating and calfing season.

The whales spend their summer in Antarctic waters where krill is abundant, then move north to winter along the southern coasts of Australia, South Africa and South America.

Southern Right Whales were first protected in 1935, when the world population was down to 1000 animals. The population is now estimated at about 2000. They are totally protected in Australian waters by Federal and State laws.

Fines up to $100 000 may be imposed for molesting or harassing whales. Boats should not approach within 100m or aircraft fly below 300 metres. A person may not swim or dive within 30m of a whale.

Southern Right Whales

Length: 15-18m
Weight: 50-96 tonnes
Swims: 3-9km/hr
Gestation: 12 months
Calfs: 5-6m at birth
Distribution: widely distributed throughout Antarctica, southern South America, Australia, New Zealand, South Africa and high latitudes of the Indian Ocean.
Visits Warrnambool: June to October

within 500m of the Merri River footbridge and limits are placed on crayfish and abalone.

Over 70 species of birds have been observed including the giant petrel, wandering albatross, muttonbirds, gulls, honeyeaters, thornbills and parrots.

Granny's Grave off Hickford Road, is a monument to Mrs James Raddleston, who died in 1848. She was the first white woman to be buried in the Warrnambool area.

Local Industries

Fletcher Jones & Staff Factory & Gardens Flaxman Street, is where the well-known Fletcher Jones range of clothing is made. Samples are sold at the factory shop. The gardens are on a former quarry site and laid out in a formal design. These gardens are always colourful and are perhaps the most photographed gardens in Victoria.

The Smith Family Warrnambool District Mill Harris Street, manufactures

Koala painted by Robert Ulmann.

St John's Presbyterian church

Customs House

Warrnambool Art gallery

the famous Warrnambool blankets. Blanket ends, woollen materials and factory seconds can be bought at the factory shop.
Open: Monday–Fri 9am–4.30pm

Botanic Gardens Situated in Botanic Road, the gardens occupy a site of 8 hectares. William Guilfoyle, Director of the Royal Botanic Gardens, Melbourne, was commissioned to design the gardens in 1877. Working with a 'howling wilderness, and rough site', he created in the 'classic style' a tranquil and beautiful park with wide curving paths, large sweeping lawns dotted with specimen trees and glimpses of water. The entrance gates have been restored and reinstated to their original position near the corner of Blomfield & Cockman Streets. The fernery was rebuilt in 1985 to original plans. The rotunda was built in 1913. Restoration of the fountain and sundial have now been completed.

Among the trees are Monterey pines (*Pinus radiata*); and Lone Pine (*Pinus brutia*) grown from seeds taken from Gallipoli, germinated in 1928, and planted at Warrnambool in 1934; Soledad pine (*Pinus torreyana*); Morton Bay figs (*Fiscus macrophylla*); Canary Island date palm (*Phoenix canariensis*); Norfolk Island pine (*Araucaria heterophylla*) and many more.

Galleries, Museums & Antiques
Performing Arts Centre Corner Liebig & Timor Streets. The foyer exhibits a superb embroidery of the City of Warrnambool, worked by members of the Embroiderers Guild, together with a magnificent tapestry of Tower Hill. The modern venue incorporates part of the original Town Hall. It houses changing art and craft exhibitions.
Open: Monday–Fri. 9am–5pm.

In House Stables Marfell Road have been tastefully restored and host a charming collection of locally made crafts. A variety of workshops are held and light lunches are always available in the gallery cafe.
Open: 10am–5pm daily

Gunditjmara Co-op Gallery Harris Reserve. The gallery houses a permanent display of Aboriginal artifacts, history and information.
Open: 9am–12am, 1pm–4.30pm

Warrnambool Art Gallery Liebig Street. This award winning structure designed by renowned architect Les Finnis houses a number of permanent collections including late 19th Century European paintings. A notable collection of Western District colonial paintings is featured along with a survey of Melbourne

modernism 1930-50 and over 600 contemporary Australian prints.
Open: 12 noon-5pm daily

Robert Ulmann's Studio. Hopkins Point Road, 4 km east of the Hopkins River Bridge. You can see this well-known wildlife artist at work in his cliff-top studio. Paintings (oils and watercolour) and sculpture are for sale.
Open most days.

Within the Warrnambool central business district there is a variety of **craft, antique and bric-a-brac** shops open during normal business hours.

Historic Buildings
Bank of Australasia (1859) at the intersection of Timor and Kepler Streets. It is now a night club.

Commercial Hotel (1856, modified to Jobbins' design in 1876) Timor Street is now the Whaler's Inn.

Court House (1871) Gilles Street.

Customs House (1860) 3 Gilles Street. It is possibly Warrnambool's earliest building, and has been restored by the South West College of TAFE as an art/craft gallery.
Open: Wednesday–Sun 11am–5.30pm.

Cramond & Dickerson Building (1855) Timor Street. The corner building on Timor and Liebig Streets was opened in 1856. Cramond & Dickerson traded in this building until 1972.

History House (1876), Gilles Street. Originally the residence of the caretaker of the saltwater baths, now the home of the Warrnambool Historical Society which has exhibits of old photographs and records from the early days of Warrnambool. Admission is charged.
Open: first Sunday in month, 2pm–4pm.

Lady Bay Hotel (1850) Pertobe Street.

Lighthouse, with cottage and store (1859), was built by W. K. Patterson, using a lantern from England.

Pair of Shops (*c*.1860), 220-2 Timor Street, are constructed of rubble limestone and have a street level facade of glazed shop-front and entry doors. The upper floor facade has matching decoration. They are probably some of the oldest commercial premises in Warrnambool.
National Bank (former) (1870s) 53 Kepler Street.

Police Station, stables, lockup and residence (1850) Gilles Street.

Sale Yards Wall (1903) (former) Spence Street is built of local sandstone.

Tower Hill

Cape Barren Geese at Tower Hill.

The layers of volcanic ash are clearly visible at Tower Hill.

A two storey **Shop & Residence** 183 Fairy Street. Many such buildings retain their dates and ornaments.

St. John's Presbyterian Church (1875) Spence Street, was constructed with local sandstone and designed by architect Andrew Kerr. A stone plaque on the front wall relates the history.

St. Joseph's Church (1872) Lava Street. Designed by George Jobbins, it replaced an earlier structure that still stands nearby. The spire was added in 1886, and shortened to its present height in 1903 after earthquake damage.

Christ Church (1854-56) Henna Street. This Anglican church was designed by architect Nathaniel Billings and is noted for its unusual double nave. The tower, designed by Andrew Kerr, was added in 1882. Other related buildings are the Rectory (1860) with its hand-sawn 12inch vertical boarding, and the later Parish Hall.

Hopkins River Boathouse (1885-1893) 2 Simpson Street. Classified by the National Trust, it is an excellent example of early Australian architecture. It is a private residence, but can be viewed from the car-park and river.

TOWER HILL

Tower Hill was formed from volcanic activity some 25,000 years ago. It was declared Victoria's first National Park in 1892, although it was not managed as such. Local action resulted in the declaration of a State Game Reserve in 1961.

Since 1961 a revegetation and native animal restocking program has returned the area to its natural state. The reserve is now rich in bird life including Cape Barren and magpie geese, ducks, spoonbills, herons, kingfishers, grey fan-tails, swamp harriers, kestrels, peregrine falcons, kites and corellas. It is also an important grouping area for many species of migratory waders prior to migration, and a feeding site for sanderlings, curlews, turnstones and sharp-tailed sandpipers.

The **Natural History Centre** houses a display depicting the areas' geology and the re-forestation program.

A 3km **scenic nature walk** will take you through the reserve. Other walks will take you to the crater rim for spectacular views of the Western District. A sealed one-way road also leads through the crater.
Open: daily (except total fire ban days)
Reserve: 8am-5pm.
Natural History Centre: 9.30am–12.30pm, 1.30pm–4.30pm.

Koroit

Koroit just north of Tower Hill has one of the most concentrated Irish descendant populations in Australia. The Catholic Church complex of buildings is impressive.

The main street is dominated by the elegant two-storey Koroit Hotel, built in 1853 from local basalt. The hotel has been in the Burke family since 1922 and offers accommodation with period decorated furnishings. The humble, intact Victorian and Edwardian shopfronts with their kerbside verandahs and the simple houses of the original settlers complete the streetscape. The commercial centre has some gracious 19th Century buildings.

The former **Tower Hill Lake National School** was built in 1858 and is an excellent example of the typical 19th Century Victorian school.

The **Botanic Gardens** were laid out in 1870s under the direction of the designer William Guilfoyle and contain seven trees that are listed on the National Register.

The **Old Courthouse Inn** was once the most popular hotel in the district and now offers bed and breakfast as well as a range of arts and craft.

A *Heritage Trail* brochure is available at Koroit.

Killarney Beach is an ideal family beach. This area is protected by reefs and is safe for swimming and small boats. The reefs are rich in bird life in particular waders and waterfowl. Camping and picnic facilities are available and the fishing is great.

Roman Catholic Catherdal, Koroit.

Historic Port Fairy from the Princes Highway. Three kilometres west of Killarney, Woodbine Road runs south and then west between Belfast Lough and the coast, crossing the Moyne River into the heart of historic Port Fairy.

Historic Woodbine Homestead, opposite the Port Fairy golf course was originally 'Lagoon Farm' when established by Charles Mills in the 1840s.

Belfast Lough is a popular windsurfing spot, exposed as it is to the coastal winds that sweep over Port Fairy Bay. The Lough is very shallow and the water often discoloured with a muddy shoreline. However, this does not discourage keen windsurfers. Access to the Lough is across the airstrip on Woodbine Road.

MARINERS
& WHALING

PORT FAIRY TO PORTLAND

Port Fairy to Portland
73 kilometres

The mysterious 'Mahogany Ship', whalers and sealers, Aboriginal village sites and fish traps, and the first permanent Victorian white settlement make this an area steeped in history.

Whaling stations were established along the shores from Port Fairy to Portland in the early 1800s. They came to plunder the oil rich seal colonies, and kill the herds of whales coming close to the shore to breed. Graziers followed close on their heels, squatting on large tracts of fertile land to establish sheep stations.

Today the seals and whales are recovering from the over hunting. The secluded gentle shoreline once again attracts nature's most fantastic sight, the spouting of a whale. The fishing industry has now replaced the whalers but Port Fairy has retained its seafaring character.

Boat Harbour on the Moyne River, Port Fairy.

PREVIOUS PAGES Cottage, Port Fairy

Seascape looking east from the Crags towards Port Fairy.

Port Fairy

Port Fairy is situated on the eastern headland of Portland Bay, at the mouth of the Moyne River. The rambling historic seaside atmosphere remains with small cottages and verandah lined streets. It was named in *c*. 1826 by Captain James Wishart, who first took his cutter, *The Fairy* across the sand-bar into the deep sheltered estuary of the Moyne River to escape a violent storm.

A few years later the abundant whales and seals attracted a tough , nomadic band of men, who hunted the defenceless Southern Right Whales and Fur-seals. It was seasonal work with the rendering or boiling down taking place on the beaches in great cauldrons. The port became one of the busiest in Australia after Sydney Harbour.

The sea was the only reliable link with the outside world. In the whaling off-season some of the boat crews were put to work building, farming or collecting wattle bark for tanning. In 1843 a large grant of land of 5120 acres (2048 hectares), was made to a Sydney solicitor, James Atkinson, 'in a parish unnamed at Port Fairy'. Atkinson laid out the town which he named Belfast, a name it held until around 1887.

Most of the building was done in the 1840s and 1850s. It virtually ceased with the collapse of Rutledge & Co in 1862. They had enjoyed a monopoly on trade in the town. William Rutledge, magistrate, stock and station agent, land magnate, grazier, business and banking adviser, also held 5120 acres of land in the vicinity of what is now, Warrnambool.

Over 50 buildings have now been classified by the National Trust, including the original whaler's cottage, the splendid wooden home of whaling skipper, Captain John Mills, and the handsome court house. The Old Caledonian Inn, built in 1844, is one of the oldest continually licensed hotels in Victoria.

AT A GLANCE
PORT FAIRY
Distance:
370km from Melbourne via Great Ocean Road 292km via Princes Highway

Tourist Information:
Visitor Information Centre
22 Bank Street,
Port Fairy Vic 3284
Phone: (03) 5568 2682

Boat Charter:
Mary S Tours and *Mulloka* conduct sightseeing and fishing trips. The ocean racing yacht *Flashdance II* offers day trips to Lady Julia Percy Island as well as 2 hour twilight cruises. All leave from the wharf, weather permitting and have blackboards stating costs and times.

Moyneyana Festival commences New Years Eve with a street procession. The festival continues over January with activities for young and old.

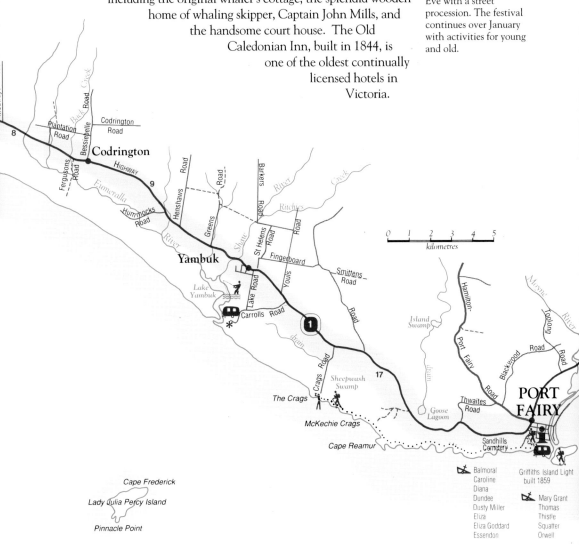

AT A GLANCE
Accommodation:
4 Motels
2 Hotels
6 Caravan Parks
3 Holiday Flats
4 Cottages

Picnic areas:
Gardens Reserve: electric barbecues.
Martins Point (Gipps Street side of the river): gas barbecues.
Mills Reserve (Griffiths Street side of the river): gas barbecues
King George Square: electric barbecues.

Places to visit:
Historical Society Museum, Gipps Street.
Mott's Cottage, Sackville Street.
Bartlett's Riverdale Art Gallery and Historic Home, 98 Gipps Street.
Griffiths Island and Pea Soup Muttonbird colonies.

Walks:
Shipwreck walk, Historic Town Walk from East Beach through the Heritage Area of Port Fairy to South Beach. The Old Port Fairy Cemetery and The Crags beach walk.

Port Fairy Folk Music Festival is held in early March each year. It is a four day celebration featuring concerts, dances, workshops, crafts, street theatre and children's folk circus.

Buildings Classified or Recorded by the National Trust

Take a walk from the junction of Gipps and Campbell Streets, following the marked route on our Port Fairy township map to take you past some of the most significant historic buildings in Port Fairy. The first is:

Merrijig Inn (1841-42) cnr Campbell & Gipps Streets. Described in the *Portland Gazette* in 1844 as the older of two first-class hotels in Port Fairy, then kept by Joseph Betts. It was the first headquarters of the whalers and later became the headquarters for the renowned 'Terrible Billy' Rutledge, squatter and magistrate. There was a large two-storey wing to the inn which was demolished in 1900. Note bluestone mile stone next to the wall- 0 miles to Belfast.

Customs House (Former) (1860-61) cnr Gipps & Campbell Streets. A bluestone structure of a domestic character with a decorative timber verandah.

Customs House

Court House (1859-60) Gipps Street. Built by John Mason, it is of bluestone construction with arcaded porch, and designed to house sittings of the Supreme Court. The interior retains its original woodwork in excellent condition.

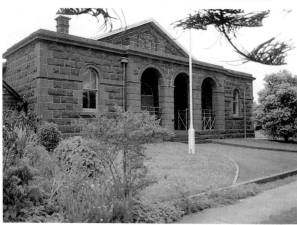

Court House

Mills Cottage (c 1840s) 40 Gipps Street. John Mills was harbour master between 1853-1871. The materials for this building were shipped from Van Diemens Land, making it one of the earliest in Port Fairy.

This cottage is believed to be the earliest building still standing in Victoria. The central weatherboard section is the oldest, built in c.1840. The rear section dates from 1847, and the front section dates from 1853. The open-work verandah posts of the cottage are unusual for Victoria where fluted and rounded columns are the rule. It is now owned by the State Government and is under restoration.

Riverside Wharf comprises warehouses and offices of the Belfast and Koroit Steam Navigation Company. The company purchased the land in 1887 and built soon after. Its steamer *Casino* was well known along the coast until wrecked in the 1930s.

'Emoh' (c.1844) 8 Cox Street. The original portion was built in 1844 for William Rutledge, who was known locally as the 'King of Port Fairy'. The Italianate front was added c 1885. Today this building serves as a Youth Hostel.

Bank of Victoria (Former) (1869) cnr Princess & Cox Streets.

Cottages-Pair (1859) 6 & 8 Princess Street.

Commercial Hotel (1850s) Bank Street. Its first licence was granted in 1852, to John Walls.

Lecture Hall & Library (1866-71) Sackville Street. They were built together for £1 340.

Star of the West Hotel (1856) cnr Bank & Sackville Streets. It was built for John Taylor, a West Indian. It was also a staging post for Cobb & Co. coaches.

Star of the West Hotel

Former **Borough Chambers** Bank Street, was the Post Office before 1881. It now serves gourmet lunches and snacks.

Dentist's Rooms (Former) (1889) 24 Bank Street.

ANZ Bank (1856) Sackville Street. (formerly Bank of Australasia) A two-storey building of half coursed basalt rock facing with emphasised quoins. It is an outstanding example of the work of architect Nathanial Billing, a noted Western District architect.

Post Office (1880-81) cnr Sackville & Cox Streets, is a fine Italianate public building.

Cottage 17 Cox Street.

©

Muttonbird Rookeries

and basalt. The corrugated iron roof covers the original slate and shingle roof. The timber verandah was built c.1915.

Mott's Cottage (c. 1845) 5 Sackville Street. It is believed that his cottage was originally built for two whalers, Mott and Stevenson. The cottage has been erected in three stages from 1845 to 1890. It has recently been restored by the National Trust and used currently as branch headquarters.

Port Fairy Post Office

Cottage (1850s) 16 Wishart Street.

Tynemouth Villa 18 Wishart Street.

Cottages (c.1855) 26-30 Campbell Street.

Cottages (1856-70) 64, 66, 68 Campbell Street. This is a group of seaman's cottages. No. 64 is a four-room bluestone cottage which is a good example of vernacular architecture. No. 66; an attic cottage still complete with its central attic dormer. It was built of local rubble limestone with basalt quoins. No. 68; a single-storey cottage built of limestone

Spring Music Festival is held in early October each year and covers the performing arts including drama, dance and innovative art.

Mott's Cottage, a National Trust property.

Caledonian Hotel

Original Milepost next to the Merrijig Inn.

Seacombe House (1847) cnr Cox & Sackville Streets. Originally the Stag Inn, it was then a school, and is now a motel.

Paired Cottages Adjacent to Seacombe House. One cottage was the first Bank of Australasia (1853), and the other the Shire Offices.

Former **Port Fairy Gazette** office (1849) Sackville Street. The paper was first printed here in 1847. Now a cafe, legal office and museum.

Caledonian Hotel (1844) cnr James & Banks Streets, was built for David McLaws, a Scottish emigrant. Licensed in 1844, it is claimed to be the oldest continuously licensed hotel in Victoria.

Braim House (c.1847) 42 James Street, this was originally a boys' boarding school run by Dr Braim.

Uniting Church 1856 James Street, was formerly the Methodist Church. There is some fine stone carving, sculptured by Walter McGill, in the porch. It is built of local basalt.

'Coombe' (1852) Regent Street. This cottage was built by R.H. Woodward. It has been restored, by one of his descendants.

St John's Church of England (1856) Church Street. Another example of the work of architect, Nathanial Billing and sculptor Walter McGill. Opened in 1856, the spire was added a century later.

'Riverdale' (1852) 98 Gipps Street, was built by John Mason, who was Captain of the Militia, and builder of the Court House and Town Hall. It now operates as Bartlett's Riverdale Art Gallery and Historic Home.

Douglas House (1852) 87 Gipps Street.

Flour Mill (1864) 75 Gipps Street, facing Bank Street. This riverside warehouse was built for Joseph Goble's flour mill. It later became a butter factory.

Other Buildings
'Girteen' (1855) 113 Griffiths Street. Built of limestone rubble it is typical of the local Georgian architecture. It is noted for its quality interior joinery.

Lighthouse (1859) Griffiths Island. Built from local quarried basalt, it stands 10.5 m above high-water level and has a fine spiral staircase and a domed metal lantern. The original light source was oil, which was later replaced by gas. It is now solar-powered and has a range of 19km.

Fortifications and Battery Hill The

lookout and flagstaff date from early settlement. The guns were installed in 1885.

Powder Magazine (1860) Battery Hill. Built by Cook & Co. the building consists of one rectangular room of bluestone with a double-brick vaulted ceiling and a corrugated-iron roof. It is situated at the entrance of the Moyne River, with its supporting coastal defence gun battery built to repel a possible invasion by the Russians in the 1850s.

St Patrick's Church Yambuk Road. (Princes Highway). The foundation stone was laid 1857 and the church consecrated in1860. It has Gothic revival architecture of rough-faced bluestone with tracery of Hobart stone and an octagonal belfry.

'Talara' Yambuk Road. (Princes Highway.) A two-storey house built of rough finished bluestone, built c.1854 in the Romantic style. It is decorated with delicate timber barge-boards and soaring finials. The building materials were imported from Britain. Today, it is well preserved with a fine interior.

'Talara'

Cottage 52 Princes Highway, noted for its turret shaped porch.

'Woodbine' (1849) Adjacent to the Port Fairy Golf Club, Woodbine was the home of Charles Mills, one of the early whaler/farmers. Many believe the first ploughing competition in Victoria was held on his property on 1 August 1854. This house was recently sold by the National Trust to decendants, Richard and Lyn Mills.

Moyne River Flour Mills (1860) at the end of Gipps Street. This mill was originally five stories high.

Museums and Galleries
Bartlett's Riverdale Art Gallery and Historic Home, 98 Gipps Street. The display includes life-sized French and Italian marble statues and an extensive collection of paintings by Australian artists. John Mason, soldier and architect built the two storey bluestone home in 1852.

Griffiths Island lighthouse

Open: Daily 9am–5pm and there is wheelchair access.
Admission is charged.

Port Fairy Historical Society Museum, now in the Court House, Gipps Street. Includes a large collection of historic photographs, personal effects and documents from prominent local citizens. *Open*: Weekends, Wednesdays and school holidays 2pm–5pm or by appointment. Admission is charged.

Shipwreck Walk At least 30 vessels were wrecked around Port Fairy between1836 and1876. Walks of 2.1km, 1.3km, and 1km have been developed by the Port Fairy Community Bicentennial Committee. They start at the surf club car-park; at Rodgers Place car-park and at Battery Lane. They all finish at Charles Mills Reserve. Each walk takes you to a vantage point overlooking a different wreck site: the barque *Socrates* (sank 30 August 1843), barque *Lydia* (ran aground 2 February 1847), schooner *Thistle* (ran aground 25 December 1837) and the brig *Essington* (beached 5 March 1852).

The Old Port Fairy Cemetery (Sandhills Cemetery) Walk
Distance: 3km return *Time*: 2 hours
Grade: easy
This is a beautiful beach walk past secluded bays to one of Victoria's oldest cemeteries. Sandhills Cemetery was opened in c 1851 and closed in1865. It is 4km west of the township just off the beach in sand dunes.

Some of the headstones have been sand blasted and partially covered by drift sand. Michael Connolly a member of Batmans Port Phillip Company is buried here. He died 12 May 1855, aged 49 years. Connolly was with Batman when he selected the site for Melbourne in 1835. He was also involved with whaling at Port Fairy. During the 1830s and 40s he exported wool. Michael Connolly is one of the forgotten pioneers who does not appear in history books.

Local historian, Les Robertson, pointing out Michael Connolly's grave.

The cemetery is only accessible from the beach, up a steep track. Start the walk at the end of Ocean Drive where a fence runs down to the beach and a management track is signposted running west. You pass two houses overlooking the first bay and round a point where a steep track climbs over the dunes to the cemetery.

At the start of the cemetery track leaving the beach you can still see the two houses passed overlooking the first bay. If the houses are out of sight you have gone too far.

Sandhills Cemetery to The Crags
Distance: 14km one way. *Time*: 8 hours
Grade: easy-medium
This walk takes you beyond the Sandhills Cemetery. It is a beach walk where you have to negotiate small cliffs and rocky headlands between long stretches of sand. The scenery is spectacular, with the rugged coastline contrasting with quiet secluded bays enclosing huge rock pools.

The walk starts at the end of Ocean Drive and heads west along the beach past Sandhills Cemetery towards Cape Reamur. There is no road access to the coast until you reach McKechnie Crags so it is advisable to carry water. It is another 3km to The Crags where a bitumen road runs north to meet the Princes Highway.

Griffiths Island
Previously referred to as Mallin or Mallone by the local Aborigines, the island is named after the whaling pioneer John Griffiths, a partner in 'Messers. Connolly & Co's Whaling Establishment', established on the island in 1836.

There were once two islands; Griffiths and Rabbit. The lighthouse was built on the then separate Rabbit Island in 1859. The single larger island was created by a breakwater and landfill. Remnants of the lighthouse moorings and gardens can be seen today. Easiest access to this area is via the river wall, then across the beach which now occupies the former gap separating the islands. A rough track is marked by pegs around the ocean side of the island and continues around the muttonbird colony to the viewing platform. Follow the marked track to protect muttonbird nests.

The Griffiths **Island Muttonbird Colony** of at least 15 000 birds creates a spectacular sight each evening, from September to April. At first there is an eerie silence as the great flocks of birds circle the island like ghosts. Then you hear a whirr of wings, later replaced by a continuous roar as the birds settle on the ground for the night. A viewing platform on the island allows visitors to watch this ritual with a minimum of disturbance to the colony. Access from the car-park is via the causeway and signposted track. A torch is useful for

Coastal sand dunes.

Fishing:
Rivers & Lakes:
Moyne River : You will catch Bream, King George Whiting, Mullet, Mulloway, Rock Cod, Salmon trout, Snapper, and Whiting.
Yambuk Lake: try for Bream, Mullet, Brown trout, Rainbow trout and Salmon trout and eels.
Fitzroy River: You can take home Bream, Mullet, Brown trout, Mulloway, Rainbow trout and Salmon trout.
Surf Fishing from the Beaches:
The Crags, East Beach, Levy's, Killarney, Yambuk and Fitzroy River mouth are excellent. Fish for Flathead, Garfish, King George whiting, Mullet, Mulloway, Salmon trout, Snapper and Trumpeter.
Bait:
You can try bluebait, clams, clinkers, crabs, craytail, earthworms, mudeyes & yabbies, sandworms, shrimp, spewworms, snails, squid and whitebait.
An amateur fishing licence is required to fish any estuary or inland water.

THE REMARKABLE MUTTONBIRD OR SHORT-TAILED SHEARWATER

Early settlers ate the bird and used it as a source of oil. For a few weeks each year the birds replaced the settlers dependence on mutton.

The birds are now protected in Victoria, although limited harvesting is still permitted by Aboriginal Communities on Cape Barren Island in Bass Strait. The Muttonbirds or Short-tailed shearwater (*Puffinus tenuirostris*) is the only member of the Petrel family who breeds on the mainland. Most colonies are on the islands around Bass Strait. The 'Pea-Soup' and 'Griffiths Island' colonies at Port Fairy are two of the rare mainland breeding areas. The 40-45cm brown-grey bird is not a great beauty but its annual migration around the Pacific Ocean, and return to its nesting burrow on the same day each year is astonishing.

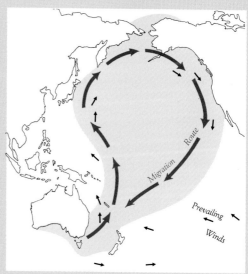

The Muttonbird's annual migration route.

Lifecycle

Between the 19 and 25 September each year, most of the breeding-age birds of the Port Fairy colony return from the northern hemisphere. Individuals relocate their old nesting burrow and the mate they have paired with for life. For the next few weeks the shallow metre long burrows dug in soft soil are cleared out. Mating takes place in early November, when the whole colony flies out to sea to feed for about two weeks.

On return a single white egg is laid. Both male and female share the incubation, with the male taking the first 12-14 day shift, the female spending the next 10-13 days in the burrow. The egg hatches mid-January. Two or three days later the chicks are left during the day while both parents hunt for food. The period grows longer as the chick gets older, with sometimes up to three weeks between meals. The parent birds are known to hunt for fish over 1 500km from the nest during this period. The chicks gain weight rapidly and for a period become heavier than the adult birds.

In mid-April as the colder windy weather sets in the adult birds begin their Pacific migration. The young are left behind. Eventually they too set off after the adults, following the annual migration path without the guidance of the older birds. Only about half those that leave the nest survive. The young birds follow a slightly later migratory timetable.

The migration takes the birds north, passing over New Zealand and Japan to spend the northern summer around the Aleutian Islands and Kamchatka Peninsula. The journey of 15 000km is completed in only two months. The adult birds leave Alaskan waters from late August to late September.

The return journey is via the coast of Alaska and California, south-west across the Pacific, around Point Hicks and into Bass Strait. For most of the journey the birds are helped by the prevailing winds, however on their final leg from the central Pacific the birds have to contend with south-east winds, returning to their nest exhausted. On the 23 September 1977, 350 000 birds were recorded crossing south-eastern New South Wales each hour.

Calendar of events of the Griffiths Island Colony

Arrival	19-25 September	Usually 22 September
Departure for mating	9-13 November	Usually 12 November
Mating at sea	11-15 days	
Return for egg laying	22-26 November	Usually 25 November
Adults depart	11-20 April	Usually 16 April
Young depart	2-9 May	Usually 3 May

Table after Miss G. Bowker (local Field Naturalist) observations 1963-1973

Muttonbird burrow on Griffiths Island

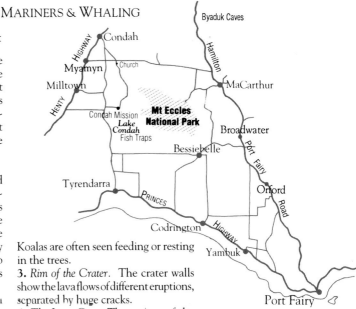

the return walk and warm protective clothing is recommended. Do not take your dogs. It is interesting to note that the greatest threat to the Muttonbirds survival is not the arduous yearly migration to the northern hemisphere, but domestic pets and foxes that prey on the young and destroy their habitat.

The 'Pea-Soup Colony' is signposted 1km west of the Griffiths Island car-park. A fenced walking track cuts through the eastern corner of the muttonbird colony where you can see the nests dug into the sand dunes at very close quarters. The track is accessible to wheelchairs. At dusk the area swarms with muttonbirds.

Pea-Soup beach is an idyllic lagoon encircled by a basalt flow. You cross a short stretch of basalt to reach the sandy beach. This is an excellent, safe beach for children to swim.

When leaving Port Fairy heading west turn left off the Princes Highway into Thistle Place immediately after 'Talara' house. There you will see a spectacular view of the coast stretching from the Port Fairy lighthouse, west to Lady Julia Percy Island and Hearn's ostrich farm. Thistle Place is a short deadend road with a turn-table.

Scenic Drive from Port Fairy to Mount Eccles National Park & Lake Condah Aboriginal Mission

Distance: 175km Time: 1 day
Take the Hamilton Road through the small settlements of Orford and Broadwater to MaCarthur. The Mount Eccles National Park is 9km south-west of the township and incorporates Mount Eccles, Lake Surprise, a dry crater, various volcanic vents, lava canals and caves.

The volcanoes erupted as recently as 19 000 years ago when a huge lava flow spewed out and hardened. It now stretches from the volcano, east to the 'Stony Rises', and ends up near the sea at Tyrendarra. Another eruption occurred 15 000 years ago when clouds of dust and ash rained down on the plains. The most recent volcanic activity was only 6 500 years ago.

Facilities at the park include picnic tables, wood barbecues and toilets. A permit is necessary for camping. Ask at the Interpretation Centre located 1km from the park entrance.

Mount Eccles Walk
Distance: 2km Time: 1hour
The track begins at the north end of the car-park and follows the rim of the crater. To make the most of the walk refer to the National Parks numbered posts. Some of the point of interest are:
1. *The Old Quarry.*
2. *Manna Gum Woodland.* This area is typical of the natural vegetation.

Koalas are often seen feeding or resting in the trees.
3. *Rim of the Crater.* The crater walls show the lava flows of different eruptions, separated by huge cracks.
4. *The Lava Cave.* The surface of the lava flow cooled first, forming a solid crust. Beneath the crust the still molten lava continued to move down hill, leaving a hollow tunnel. Over time part of the crust collapsed, exposing the 60m tunnel, or cave, beneath.
5. *Lava Canal.* This is another example of a formation produced by a hardened crust of lava with the molten lava underneath draining away. In time, the roof of the tunnel collapsed leaving the canal as we see today. The canal shows the route the lava took during the last eruption of the volcano. A rough walking track, of 4 hours return, follows the canal.
6. *Lake Surprise* has a maximum depth of 14m and is fed by underground springs. The lake actually occupies three craters.
7. *View of Mount Eccles.* It was formed when westerly winds blew scoria from the crater to form the dome. Molten lava from the next eruption then coated the slopes. Some lava solidified to form the basalt we see today, while other rock fell from the cone, leaving the huge holes visible near the summit.
8. *Saddle between the craters.* With your back towards Lake Surprise you can look down along a line of dry-bed craters and a series of volcanic vents.
9. *Mount Eccles is 198m high.* It is one of several western district volcanoes whose

Byaduk Lava Caves
Church Cave, one of the most spectacular caves in the area, is situated 11km north of MaCarthur on the Hamilton Road. It is located in a Crown Land reserve east of the bitumen road. From the surface there is little to see, however when you look down into the circular entrance a profusion of tree and ground ferns can be seen within the protected entrance chamber. A walking track leads down into the cave where huge blocks of basalt are strewn on the floor. Take a torch if you intend exploring the inner recesses of the cave.

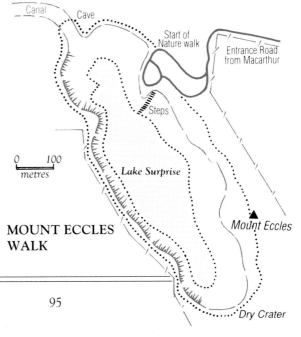

MOUNT ECCLES WALK

Lake Surprise and the National Park bushland.

Ruins of Lake Condah Mission

rock has weathered to produce the rich soils for the surrounding plains. Watch your step on the loose scoria when walking down the hill.

After leaving the National Park drive back towards MaCarthur for 3km and then north for 4km to pick up the MaCarthur-Myamyn Road.

The turnoff to the **Lake Condah Aboriginal Mission Tourist Development** is about 15km west. Turn left (south) immediately you pass the Church of England. It is another 8km to Lake Condah Aboriginal Mission Tourist Development and the ruins.

The Mission

The Lake Condah Mission operated between the 1860s and 1919 as a home for the dispossessed Kerrup-jmara people. Today part of the mission reserve has been returned to the Aborigines who have established an interpretative and accommodation centre where they conduct tours to the nearby traditional stone house relics, fish traps, and corroboree circle. The fish traps are some of the marvels of surviving Aboriginal engineering work, and the stone house sites show how traditional village life was.

Lake Condah and surrounding area are on the western volcanic plains formed when Mt Napier and Mt Eccles erupted some 19 000 years ago. The shallow lake is 4km long and 1km wide, formed at the edge of the lava flow. The Aboriginal owners were the Kerrup-jmara clan of the Gournditch-jmara tribe. They made their extensive fish and eel traps from the local volcanic

stone which harnessed the natural flooding of the lake to activate the traps.

Fish Traps At the lake there are four major trap systems. They consist of canals and low stone-walls designed to guide fish and eels into nets made of plaited grasses or bark. The nets had small exits so the fish and eels emerging could be caught easily by the waiting hunters.

The Eels life cycle Eels live most of their lives in streams and lakes, and when sexually mature they migrate downstream, sometimes even across country, to the ocean. They then swim huge distances to their breeding grounds in northern Australian and New Caledonian waters. There they descend to 200-300 fathoms, spawn and die. The eggs float to the surface and the young hatch into thin, transparent fish like creatures. In this larval stage they float south. When about 80mm long, and a dark colour, they seek fresh water streams entering the ocean, and swim up-stream. These 'elvers' can climb steep slippery rocks, waterfalls and cataracts, to reach locations not accessible to other fish. They then live out their lives in the fresh water streams, dams and reservoirs until they reach sexual maturity, when the cycle is repeated.

Close to Lake Condah are the remains of semi-circular stone dwellings, made of local volcanic rock. These buildings were sited on high ground with their door way (from floor to roof) facing away from the wind. Roofing material was probably branches and bark.

Aborigines

Europeans arrived in the area in 1841 and took over the Gournditch-jmara lands. In the 1860s a mission was established at Darlot Creek near Lake Condah, by the Church of England. A reserve of 2043 acres was set aside in 1869, and a further 1710 acres was added in 1885. In 1889 the Aboriginal population at the mission reached its maximum of 117 people. The Aborigines Protection Law Amendment Act forced the part-Aboriginal family members under the age of 35 years to leave the older people at the mission while they

STREAM
FLOW

Fish trap in position within the stone lined canal.

Reed and grass eel trap was approximately 2m in length.

Freshwater Eel   *Reed and grass fish trap*

had to 'assimilate into European society'. As a result by 1889 the population had dwindled, land ownership was revoked, and the mission slowly declined until 1919, when it was closed. Much of the balance of the land was parceled out to returning soldiers of World War 2.

Mt Napier, a small yet distinctive volcanic scoria cone dominates the horizon to the north of Mt Eccles. A walking track leads to the crater and summit where you get panoramic views spanning from the Grampians around to Portland and the Southern Ocean. Access is from the Mt Napier Road, north of Byaduk on the Hamilton - Port Fairy Road. A signposted track leads to the picnic site at the base of the summit.

The Crags 12km west of Port Fairy is a popular rocky foreshore with calcified plant roots and a view of Lady Julia Percy Island. The Crags is also a popular skin-diving spot.

Yambuk
The Yambuk Inn is a local landmark on the Princes Highway with its bluestone construction and it's distinctive attic windows.

Lake Yambuk A camping ground and boat ramp are on the eastern side of the lake estuary and reached by turning south from the Princes Highway along either Carolls or Lake Roads. The Shaw and Eumeralla Rivers discharge into the shallow lake which opens into the Southern Ocean. The lake is suitable for small craft and the bream and mullet fishing is exceptional. It is a short distance to Yambuk surf beach from the camping ground where you get a clear view of Lady Julia Percy Island. A popular attraction for children is the giant slide which runs down a sand dune next to the camping and picnic reserve. Take a bag to sit on and get the ride of a life time.

Lady Julia Percy Island Lying 19km off the coast Lady Julia Percy Island is awe-inspiring. It is unapproachable in rough weather.

First sighted by European seamen in the early 1800s, the island was named by Lieutenant James Grant, captain of the supply vessel *Lady Nelson*.

Lady Julia Percy Island was formed during two periods of volcanicity, the first left the 'boulder tuff', the later eruptions left the dense basalt. The island is the same age as Tower Hill, formed some one million years ago in the upper Pleistocene period.

The island rises 46m above sea level. Depressions on the island are probably caused by collapsing underground lava

tunnels. The shallow soil is rich and black and supports bracken fern and grasses.

Bird life: Lady Julia Percy Island is a naturalist's paradise, with fairy penguin and muttonbird colonies. It also has the largest rookeries of fairy prions and diving petrels in Australia. The birds shelter beneath boulders on the talus slopes in Dingy Cove. Dotterels, peregrine falcons, kestrels, swamp harriers, swallows, chats, and pipits also make the island their home, along with fairy penguins. The penguins are small sturdy birds, blue-black on the back and white on the chest and belly. They nest in burrows at the western end of the island. After a day fishing at sea they assemble at Seal Bay before coming ashore at dusk. They take about an hour to climb up to the plateau for the night. At day break they descend again to the sea.

Seals: The seals were near extinction in the mid 19th Century, but numbers have now risen to over 4000. They gather on the rocks and beaches of the island, in particular on the western shore. Bulls, seals and pups of varying ages and sizes can be seen lying among the rocks, except during the breeding season.

The noise of the seal colony is loud and incessant ranging from the hoarse coughing of the bulls to the higher-pitched grunts of the females and the sheep-like bleating of the pups. Clumsy on land, the seals are acrobats in the water. You can watch their skill for hours as they hunt for barracouta, parrot-fish, crabs and squid along the margins of the kelp beds off the island.

A charter boat takes visitors from Port Fairy to Lady Julia Percy Island, or you can look out to the island from The Crags or from the beach at Lake Yambuk .

The Fitzroy River Outlet. Follow Thompsons Road south from the Princes Highway to the Fitzroy River boat ramp and bush camping area.

The boat ramp and jetty provide access for fishermen with small craft wanting to fish for bream up stream and along the estuary. Picnic facilities and pit toilets are provided. A walking track follows the eastern side of the estuary to the ocean beach, accessible at low tide. It is a safe swimming beach for children.

Narrawong
A small coastal town, Narrawong is sited on the mouth of the Surry River. Clarke Street runs beside the estuary and terminates in a car-park where a fenced walking track leads to the beach. From the beach is an excellent view across Portland Bay to Portland Aluminium Smelter.

On the western side of the estuary is

View from The Crags to flat-topped Lady Julia Percy Island

Seals off Lady Julia Percy Island.

• WHALES & WHALING •

Hunting whales was the most dangerous of seafaring activities. Some of the whales were over 20m in length and weighed as much as 25 elephants. The whales were an energy source for 19th Century Europe. They provided oil for lamps and wax for candles. The flexible slender whalebones were also used for corsets, umbrellas and the hoops beneath womens' long dresses.

The first recorded British whaler to hunt in the south Pacific was the *Emilia*. With her triumphant return to London in 1790 and the reported catch, the great Pacific whale and seal hunt was on.

The establishment of the first convict settlement at Sydney provided the whalers with a safe harbour and port for restocking provisions. As early as 1791 sperm whales were killed off the coast from Sydney. Between 1800 and 1806 eighteen British whalers called at Sydney with seal oil, skins and 2800 tuns [whale oil measure, one tun was equal to about 955 litres or 210 imperial gallons] of sperm oil. This was worth £200 000 in 1806 values, a huge sum of money.

With the establishment of the Hobart convict settlement in 1803 the whalers were able to be supplied closer to the hunting grounds of Bass Strait, and the industry expanded rapidly.

Many mainland whaling stations had been established in Tasmania and the south coast of Victoria by the 1820s. The whales preferred shallow inshore waters in winter. Their slow swimming speed meant they could be rowed down in places like Portland Bay and Lady Bay at Warrnambool.

The intensity of the combined off-the-beach and ocean hunting in Australasian waters killed more that 12 000 Southern Right Whales in the five years between 1835-1839. The number dropped to 7000 over the next five years. Whale numbers were so depleted that operations eventually ceased. The Southern Right Whale had been hunted close to extinction, and has remained a rare animal ever since.

Types of whales hunted

The Sperm Whale was once common along the coastline, but its numbers have never recovered from the hunting decimation. It has a long barrel-shaped body with a squared head almost one third of the total body length. A long narrow lower jaw has 18 to 25 large conical teeth

An American Whaler.

which fit into sockets on the top jaw. The pectoral fins are small and broad. The colouring is light-brown to blue-grey and the skin rippled on the back and sides. Males average 18.5m in length and weigh 32 to 45 tonnes, calves are 3.7m to 4.3m at birth. Their diet consists of squid, fish, and octopus and they live for up to 70 years.

Southern Right Whales These are the whales which are returning to the southern coast. They are a large black whale, up to 18m in length, with white callosities around the head and mouth. They have a smooth finless back and deeply-notched tail flukes which are held clear of the water when the whale 'sounds' or dives. Refer to page 83 for more detail on the Southern Right Whale.

Whalers and whaleboats Their ships were generally 300 to 400 tonnes and carried a crew of 28 to 35 men. Each vessel carried six whaleboats. On board the conditions were cramped, and the work exhausting. When the whales were 'blowing' the crew ate and slept in the forecastle. Their wooden bunks were arranged in two tiers along the sides of the ship towards the bow. The head height was minimal.

Near the middle of the ship were the quarters for the harpooners, the long-boat steerer, the steward and the cooper, who made the sperm oil barrels. The highest and better cabins were occupied by the mates, with the state-room, occupied by the ship's master, and sometimes his wife.

Whaleboats: Each whaleboat had a crew of six men. These were about 9m in length by 1.5m in width; and pointed at both ends so they could sail or row in either direction without turning. Near one end was a strong, upright, rounded piece of wood, called the 'loggerhead'; at the other was the 'head' which had a groove cut exactly in the centre through which the harpooners' rope ran out. Each whaleboat had two lines of rope, at least 400m in length, coiled in tubs ready for use, three or four harpoons, two or three lances, a keg containing a lantern and tinder-box, two or three

Size comparison of a Sperm, Southern Right whale and man.

Reconstructed, Australian designed, whaleboat at the Flagstaff Hill Maritime Village, Warrnambool.

flags and two or three 'drouges'. These were pieces of board attached to the line to drag through the water and help slow down the harpooned whale.

Hunting whales at sea

Whalers stationed lookouts on each of the mast-heads, and an officer at the fore-top-galley-yard. When a whale was spotted the call 'there she spouts' or 'there she blows' was given and the ship would come to life. If the whale was to leeward the ship was brought to within 400m, but if to the windward the whaleboats were sent in chase. These chases could last a few hours or a day.

The whaleboat was rowed as close as possible to the whale and the harpoon with rope attached thrown. Once the whale was struck, the line was looped two or three times around the loggerhead. The whale then dragged them with the boat steerer guiding the boat with an oar passed through a ring attached to the 'gummet'. He also attended to the line. The headsman then went forward and prepared to plunge his lance to kill the whale.

Once killed, the whale was towed back to the whaler or onto the beach to be cut up, and boiled down. The oil was run off into barrels to be transported to world-wide destinations.

While whaling was a cruel and shortsighted industry which drove the animals close to extinction, it was also a tough and very dangerous life for the men and many Aboriginal women who were captured and forced to live with and assist their whaling captors.

In the late 1970s, world sympathy for whales was mobilised, and pressure applied to the last few whaling stations. Only Japan now continues to hunt whales, mainly for eating.

Since 1980 Australia has banned all whaling within 400km of the coast and has banned any Australian nationals from working on foreign whaling ships.

Once again our coastline provides a safe haven for the magnificent whale.

the Narrawong Camping and Recreation Reserve. There is an excellent bathing area for children in the river mouth shallows adjacent to the main camping area.

Fishing from Narrawong Beach and the Surry River which encircles the reserve is always good.

An artesian bore provides hot water for the amenities blocks. The water hits the surface at 58°C and is rich in iron and sulphur. The bore was drilled in 1969 to a depth of 1700m.

The Narrawong Cemetery off Boyers Road, north of the Princes Highway has the grave of Captain William Dutton, Master Mariner, Portland Bay 1828-78.

Narrawong State Forest North of the Princes Highway is 400 000 hectares of forest. The timber ranges from messmate, swamp gum, peppermint and manna gum to brown stringy bark. The area was first explored by Edward Henty in 1834, when he climbed the nearby Mt Clay (190m). Two years later Major Mitchell passed through on his way to Portland. The hardwood forests supplied the sawn timber for the whaling stations at Portland. They are now a remnant of what once covered the coast. Eight thousand hectares are now pine plantations. The forest is traversed by good all-weather roads and picnic areas are located at the Sawpit and Surry Ridge.

Sawpit Picnic Area & Whalers Lookout Situated in the Narrawong State Forest, off Boyers Road. Within the picnic area, set amongst stringybark, the original saw pit has been preserved and reconstructed by the Department of Conservation and Environment. Here you can see how the timber for the early buildings of Portland was sawn.

Whalers Lookout In the early days signal fires were lit on the Surry Hills to signal the sighting of whales. A 15 minute walk from the car-park takes you to the summit and lookout. The surrounding messmate forests harbour a number of native animal and bird species.

Surry Ridge Picnic Area Just past Heathmere, turn left into Coffey's Lane from the Portland—Heywood road, and follow the track to the picnic area. Here you can see fine river vegetation, blackwood and manna gums. Two walks to Surry Gorge and Hodgett's Grove are sign posted. Picnic facilities include tables, wood barbecues and water.

Leaving the Princes Highway

Keillers Road runs south from the Princes Highway past Narrawong. It joins Dutton Way which skirts the shoreline of Portland Bay and finally takes you into the heart of Portland.

Pit sawing
The top sawyer walked backwards along the top of the log being cut, pulling the saw upwards and then steering it on its downward stroke. The pitman walked fowards, pulling the saw down on the cutting stroke. The teeth of the saw were away from the pitman, so not as much sawdust fell on him as might be expected. The saws ranged in length from 1.75m to 2m.

Handle

Tiller

Handle

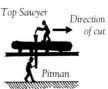

Top Sawyer

Direction of cut

Pitman

ALONG THE
DISCOVERY COAST

PORTLAND TO NELSON

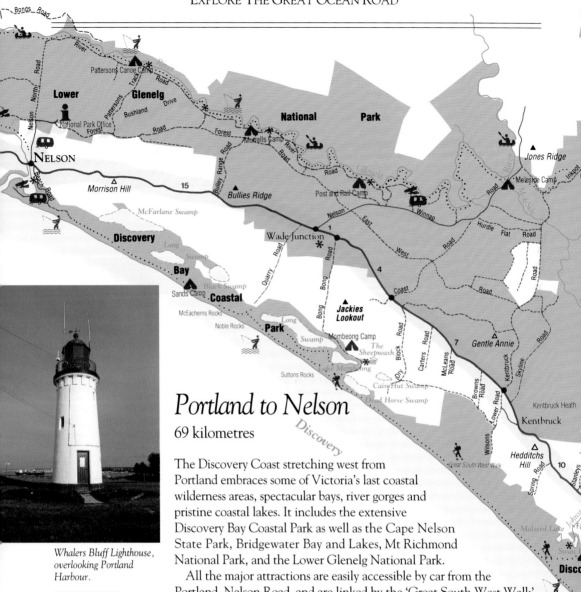

Whalers Bluff Lighthouse,
overlooking Portland
Harbour.

PREVIOUS PAGES
The Glenelg River

Massive bulk carriers link
the region to world
markets.

Portland to Nelson

69 kilometres

The Discovery Coast stretching west from
Portland embraces some of Victoria's last coastal
wilderness areas, spectacular bays, river gorges and
pristine coastal lakes. It includes the extensive
Discovery Bay Coastal Park as well as the Cape Nelson
State Park, Bridgewater Bay and Lakes, Mt Richmond
National Park, and the Lower Glenelg National Park.

   All the major attractions are easily accessible by car from the
Portland–Nelson Road and are linked by the 'Great South West Walk',
a 250km walking track. Don't forget to include some good walking shoes
so you can explore the numerous short walking tracks designed to take in
the areas best features. You can also canoe the Glenelg River Gorge and
climb the massive mobile sand dunes fringing Discovery Bay or venture
underground into the Princess Margaret Rose Caves.

Portland

Portland is a modern city with 12 000 people and is the only deep-sea port between Melbourne and Adelaide serving inland south-eastern Australia. Historically, the port was first visited by trading vessels in the 1820s, but all traces of the facilities that serviced ships in the 19th century have since been obliterated by a modern port. Free tours of the port allow visitors to view shipping activities close up. Phone 03 5523 2671 for details. Major industries dependent on the port include abattoirs, fertilizer processors, sawmilling, aluminium smelting, fishing and woolstores.

The Portland Aluminium Smelter is one of the biggest single investments in Victorian resources and produces about 320 000 tonnes of aluminium ingot for export each year. The smelter is surrounded by a combination of wildly beautiful coast, natural heathland and farmland.

AT A GLANCE
PORTLAND
Distance:
439 km from Melbourne via The Great Ocean Road.
362km from Melbourne via Princes Highway.

Tourist Information:
Portland Visitor Information Centre
Cliff Street,
Portland Vic 3305
Phone: (03) 5523 2671
Toll Free: 1800 035 567

Accommodation:
10 Motels
5 Caravan Parks
4 Bed & Breakfast

Picnic Spots:
Electric BBQ's and tables at: *Battery Point* on Portland Bay, *Lions Club Nature Park* off Bridgewater Road, *Ploughed Field* opposite hospital, *Clifftop* off Hanlon Parade and *Henty* and *Nuns Beach*. *Fawthrop Lagoon* situated between the city and south Portland also has walking tracks, barbecue and picnic facilities.

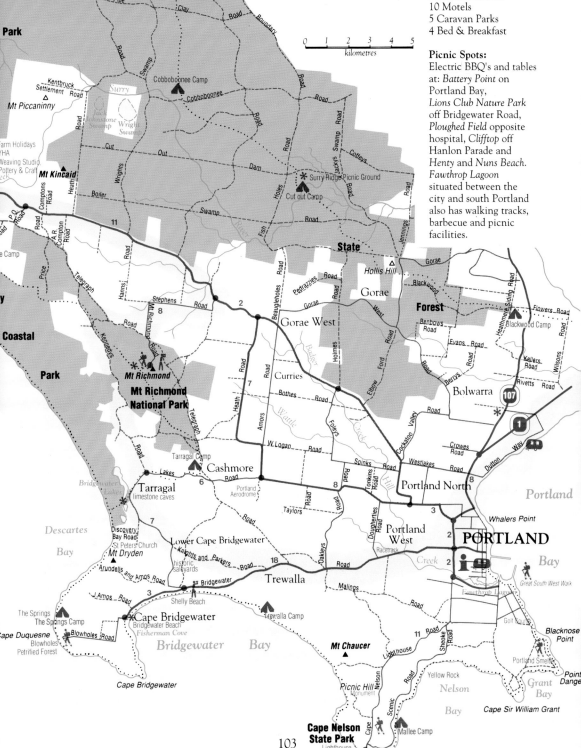

Places to Visit:
Cape Nelson State Park, Bridgewater Bay, Blowholes, Petrified Forest, Bridgewater Lakes and Caves, and Mt Richmond National Park

Walks:
Smelter Nature Walk

Bird watching:
Lawrence Rocks An important breeding ground for several seabirds, including the Australian Gannet, Fairy Penguins, Fairy Prion, Sooty Oystercatcher and Short-tailed Shearwater.

Fishing:
Jetties, piers and wharfs
Rock Cod, Sweep, Snapper, Whiting, Flathead, Trevally and Silver Trevally. Some wharfs are closed to the public when ships are berthed.
Bay
Salmon, Snapper, Barracouta, Flathead, Whiting and in January, Yellowtail Kingfish.

Surfing:
Blacknose Point Point break, good fun hot-dog waves for experienced surfers and novices (watch the rocks). Best during heavy swell, or SE swell and S-SW wind.
Crumpets Point break, good fun hot-dog wave for experienced and beginners. Needs W-SW wind with moderate swell.
Yellow Rock Fast breaking powerful waves on sand and rock floor. Needs N-NW wind with low swell. Dangerous currents at times and should only be attempted by experienced surfers.

In 1800 the British Admiralty instructed Sydney bound Lieutenant James Grant to try and sail from England through the recently-discovered Bass Strait from the west, instead of taking the usual route around Van Diemen's Land (Tasmania). He succeeded and cut weeks off the arduous journey. On the way Grant named most of Victoria's coastal features including Capes Banks, Bridgewater, Nelson, Liptrap, Otway and Schank. He also named Mt Gambier, Portland Bay, and most of the islands around Wilsons Promontory. Portland Bay was named after the Duke of Portland.

These waters received little attention until sealers and whalers extended their search for new sources of oil from Van Diemen's Land. Whaling stations soon appeared on Portland Bay once word got out about the large number of whales that migrated to Portland Bay each year.

Captain William Dutton, the most famous of these whalers, built a house near where the Harbour Trust Offices stand today. His grave is in the Narrawong Cemetery east of Portland.

The original Henty Woolstore

The Henty family is credited with establishing Victoria's first permanent European community in Portland in 1834. Two years later, Major Mitchell was stunned to find a comfortable white family in its homestead with thriving flocks and herds at the end of his epic journey to 'unknown parts'.

Portland is the largest live sheep export centre in eastern Australia.

Yachts make a blaze of colour on Henty Beach.

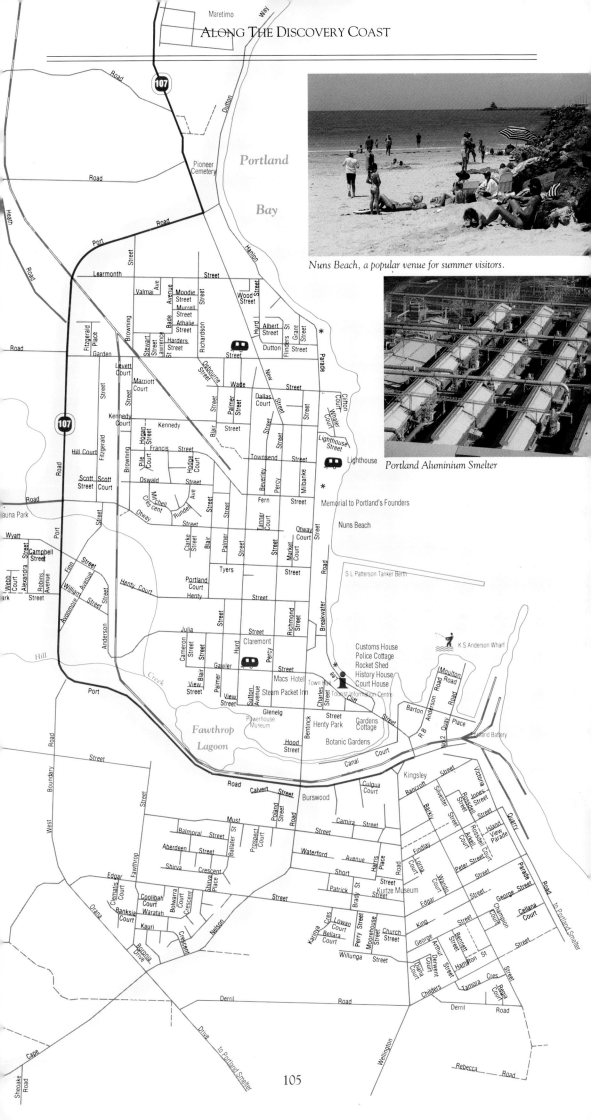

Nuns Beach, a popular venue for summer visitors.

Portland Aluminium Smelter

Portland has over 200 historic buildings dating from the 1880's. These include two Henty bluestone mansions, 'Burswood' and 'Claremont'.

Portland Battery built on Battery Point in 1889 to repel a feared Russian invasion is one of three Western Batteries (Warrnambool, Port Fairy and Portland). The magazine and Lamp Passage are accessible by a 5 metre ladder. A small collection of photographs and rifles is on display. As part of Portlands 150th anniversary celebrations in 1984, three cannons were restored and the area landscaped. Battery Point overlooking Portland Bay is an excellent picnic spot with electric barbecues and ample car parking. *Guided tours* are conducted 2pm to 4 pm during weekends and holidays.

Court House, Cliff Street.

Court House c.1845, Cliff Street. It was one of the first major government buildings erected in south-western Victoria. Built of bluestone on a slight rise overlooking the harbour, it is of a simple classical form and has a close relationship with the other early buildings in the vicinity.

The Monument opposite 143 Bentinck Street, erected in 1914, commemorates Portland's founders including Lieutenant James Grant, Captain William Dutton, the Henty Brothers and Major Mitchell. The site is significant because it is the spot where the Henty's planted Victoria's first commercial wheat crop in September 1835. **Cast iron whale boilers** used to boil down whale blubber were added in 1978 to commemorate the centenary of William Dutton's death.

Hidden behind trees overlooking Portland Harbour is the bluestone mansion **Maretimo** built by grazier and politician J.N.McLeod in 1859. The house is situated on the Dutton Way.

Burswood, 15 Cape Nelson Road, was built in 1855 by Edward Henty and designed by colonial architect, John Barrow. Dressed bluestone and brick are the dominant building materials and

the interior features hand made glass and timber panelling imported from England.

Steam Packet Inn (1842) 33 Bentinck Street, was prefabricated in Tasmania and built by Robert Herbertson. The two story weather-board building is one of Victoria's oldest hotels with its hipped roof and dormer windows, reflecting an earlier building style. Also known as a *'house of ill fame'* in the 1850s, the Inn spent its last occupied years as a private residence.
Open: Thursdays and Sundays: 2pm–4pm. December to June.

Steam Packet Inn, Bentinck Street.

Customs House Cliff Street, built in 1849 is the oldest government building still in use. This imposing example of colonial architecture has a strong Tasmanian influence.

Kingsley (1893) 50 Bancroft Street, is probably Portland's most visible historic building as it dominates the sky line above the port . The two storied weather-board house, complete with tower is the head office with cellar sales for Kingsley Wines whose main vineyard is situated at Gorae West.

The **Botanic Gardens** were laid out on eight hectares of land in 1854 and reduced in size when the harbour was constructed during the 1950s. Don't miss seeing the **Curators Cottage** in the Botanic gardens, built in 1860 and now restored and refurbished. Alongside the gardens is the **lifeboat** used to rescue 19 survivors of the *Admella* in 1859.

Curators Cottage, Botanic Gardens.

At the former **Town Hall,** now 'History House' in Charles Street, an outstanding collection of early photographs shows the town and its people from the 1840s to 1930s. In 1984 part of the Historical Society's Collection was added to this display, together with records from the Genealogical Group, and microfilms of early Portland newspapers, to make 'History House' a museum and historical resource centre.

Power House Museum, corner of Glenelg and Percy Streets, is a motoring memorabilia centre, featuring an impressive collection of veteran, vintage and classic cars, motorcycles and tractors.

Exhibitions include a massive 10-tonne Ruston Hornsby engine made in 1933, which saw 20 years service of generating electricity and a further 18 years powering a sawmill.Other highlights are antique signs, petrol pumps, garage equipment and restored engines.
Open: Weekdays 1pm–5pm and 10am–5pm weekends, public and school
holidays.

Portland Smelter Portland Aluminium is actively working to protect the natural beauty and to restore the surrounding agricultural land, on their 470 ha site, to parkland capable of attracting, and providing refuge for native animals. The dominant features of the smelter are the huge circular storage bins for alumina, the coke storage silos, the four parallel potrooms each about 750 metres long, the switch yard to handle power supplies and the overhead alumina conveyor system. The smelter is situated in Quarry Road and guided tours of this unique operation are conducted on Tuesday afternoons. Bookings can be made through the Portland Visitor Information Centre or by phoning (03) 5523 2671.

Smelter Nature Walk
Located just south of Portland is a 2.3 km section of the Great South West Walk which has been sealed and contoured to cater for visitors with limited mobility including those in wheelchairs. Serviced by car-parks at each end of its extent and with regular resting places along its length, the Smelter Nature Walk is a must for all, with its spectacular scenery and detailed plant descriptions which add to your understanding and enjoyment.

A **Fur Seal colony** of over 600 seals can be reached from the rest area located up the hill past the **Portland Surf Life Saving Club** some twenty kilometres out from Portland on the Cape Bridgewater Road. It is an energetic two hour return walk, but definitely worth the effort.

Rocket Shed Cliff Street, was built in 1887 and used to house rockets and beaching buoy equipment to rescue survivors from shipwrecks and recover cargo. It now displays mementos of Portland's 150th anniversary celebrations.

Pioneer Cemetery overlooking Portland Bay, off the Henty Highway, was opened in 1841 and closed in 1883. A wander through the graves while reading the headstones gives an insight to the early history of Portland.

Portland Smelter surrounded by parkland.

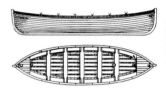

Life boats were clinker built and ranged in length from 8.5 to 10m, with 10 oars double banked. The boats were double ended. By the 1860s and 70s lifeboats were stowed in the upright position with the boats resting in chocks on skid beams. The boats were then slid outwards to the davits, for lowering into the water.

Light weight Rocket Lines were fired from the shore to a distressed ship. A heavier line was attached, and pulled on board the ship by the crew.

Cape Nelson State Park

Craggy coastal cliffs, a lighthouse, sea birds and the unusual Soap Mallee unique to Cape Nelson are some of the attractions in the 210 ha **Cape Nelson State Park** . It is situated 11 km south-west of Portland along the sealed Cape Nelson road. You can make the round trip to Portland via the Norman Wade Scenic Drive which skirts Nelson Bay.

A picnic area with fireplaces, picnic tables and toilets is signposted off the Norman Wade Scenic Drive 1 km east of the Cape Nelson Road.

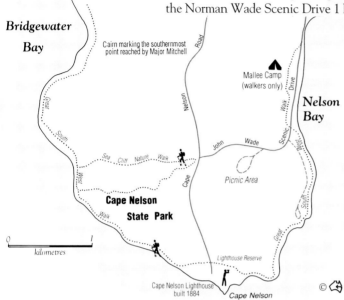

From Yellow Rock, looking east to Cape Grant.

Fishing:
Cape Nelson
Locals do fish off the rocks around Cape Nelson, but remember that rock fishing can be dangerous. Watch out for big seas and the incoming tide.
Bridgewater Bay
Salmon, Mulloway, Flathead, Sweep, and sharks.

Bird watching
Small communities of Rufous Bristlebird, Emu Wren, Tawny-crowned Honeyeater, Ground Parrot, Emu and some species of quail.

The **Cape Nelson Lighthouse** , built in 1884 is one of the popular scenic attractions in the park. One hundred and twenty nine steps rise 23 metres to the beacons which can be seen 35km out at sea. Contact Portland Visitor Information Centre for lighthouse opening times where you can photograph the distinctive white residence, stores, rocket house, and signal mast which surround it.

The **Sea Cliff Nature Walk** and the **Great South West Walk** which pass through Cape Nelson Park provide excellent easy walking.

The **nature walk** is 3km long and takes 1.5 to 2 hours to complete at a leisurely pace. It starts at the car-park near the junction of the Cape Nelson Road and Norman Wade Scenic Drive. It has numbered points of interest described in track notes available at the start of the walk which give an introduction to the natural history of the area. You can watch sea and land birds, kangaroos, echidnas, snakes and lizards. Do not forget to include binoculars. Note the limestone, laid down in an ancient sea, overlying the basalt of the rock platforms near sea level.

Flat-topped Lady Julia Percy Island is also clearly visible on the horizon.

Bridgewater Bay & Cape Bridgewater

The Bridgewater Road leads you out of Portland, through small farms broken here and there by patches of coastal heath that once covered the entire area. These gradually give way to larger properties with cleared hills, rolling away to sand dunes that mark the coastline.

Approximately 16km out of Portland look for the sign to **Shelly Beach** almost opposite the Bridgewater Lakes turn-off. Drive into the parking area in the sand dunes and take the short walk to the beach where the view in both directions is breathtaking. The rocky outcrops including **Bishop's Rocks** and **Flat Rock** are favourite fishing spots, but take care as large seas can sweep away the unsuspecting fisherman. The beach here also yields lucky finds for shell collectors.

Drive another 3 km to **Bridgewater Beach** which ends under the protective cliffs of Cape Bridgewater. The Cape breaks the persistent south-westerly winds and together with the gently shelving beach creates the long sets of rolling surf which have made the area famous. The bay is home for the Portland Surf Life Saving Club which hosts the Admella Surf Boat Marathon each November. The waves are also excellent for wave riders and surf skis. Don't forget your wet suit however, as the water can be quite cool even during the summer months.

Up the hill past the Life Saving Club is a rest area, one of the highest points on the Victorian coastline with views back towards Cape Nelson. Another 3km along Blowholes Road is a car-park on Cape Duquesne. Immediately ahead, 100 metres away are the blowholes. The best time to see these in action is during rough seas or storms during the winter months.

Blowholes

The blowholes are rock tunnels carved by the sea action along joints in the soft volcanic rock of the area. Waves crash into the tunnels, compressing the trapped air. When the wave energy is spent the air expands, shooting a spout of water high into the air.

Petrified Forest

A few minutes walk from the Blowholes car-park is the petrified forest. As you follow the track towards the sea cliff this strange formation can be seen rising from the yellow coloured limestone. The shapes are the remains of an enormous forest which once covered many square kilometres. All that is preserved today are the trunks and roots of the trees, which look like the ruins of an ancient city silhouetted against the sea. The trees were preserved in limestone in the growing position, so you can see how closely they grew, and finally died.

As the winds blows from the ocean the stumps are gradually being eroded away, exposing the roots. Over much of the area, only a slightly raised ring is left on the ground, marking the outer bark and the wood of the trees. Be careful not to damage the formations and keep to the walking track.

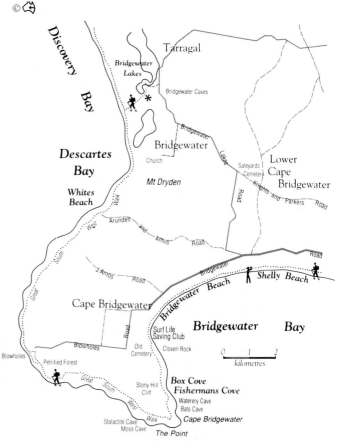

Petrified Forest.

Another walking track leads west from the blowholes car-park to a spring on the wave platform at the base of the cliff. The fresh water pool fed by the spring has been used by native game and cattle during droughts. The animals must have been extremely sure footed to negotiate the rugged descent. The return walk is about 4km in length.

There are a number of similar springs in the area. Surface water soaking through the limestone is stopped by the underlying basalt and flows between the layers to emerge as springs.

After you have explored the Cape return to Bridgewater Beach and turn left at the Lakes Road. Two kilometres from the turn-off is the settlement of **Bridgewater**. St Peter's Church, an early English gothic-style church, built in 1884 dominates the scene. It is classified and restored by the National Trust. The cemetery, saleyards and fire brigade shed are all that remain of Bridgewater.

At several points along this road there are excellent views of the **Bridgewater Lakes** and the sand dunes bordering **Discovery Bay** to the west. The entrance to **Bridgewater Lakes** is another 4km along this road. Opposite the entrance you will see limestone caves running along a small ridge on your right. A short walk up the hill takes you to the caves.

Over looking the Bridgewater Lakes from the limestone caves opposite.

The **Bridgewater Lakes** have fresh water with no outlet to the sea. They are popular for swimming, sailing, water-skiing, boating, and fishing. There is a walking track leading to the ocean beach and excellent picnic facilities. On the Main Lake, fishing and water-skiing are allowed at certain specified times of the day. The Lakes are part of the Discovery Bay Coastal Park.

Mount Richmond National Park

Mt Richmond can be reached by continuing north from the Bridgewater Lakes along Kennedy's Road or by following the Nelson Road from Portland for 16.2km to the National Park turn off on your left.

The park offers good secluded individual barbecue facilities with fresh water, tables and firewood. Kangaroos and wallabies are often the only intruders to share your picnic site. Delightful short walks take you to vibrant wild flower displays during Spring and different types of trees and shrubs. Koalas can often be seen feeding on manna gums along the tracks. A lookout tower provides views of Discovery Bay and on a clear day the Grampians (Gariwerd) are visible.

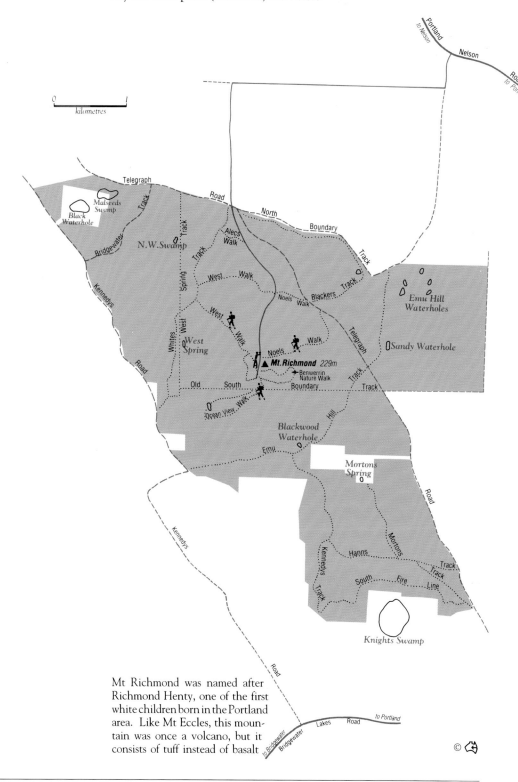

Mt Richmond was named after Richmond Henty, one of the first white children born in the Portland area. Like Mt Eccles, this mountain was once a volcano, but it consists of tuff instead of basalt and is now covered by a layer of sand, blown inland long ago from Discovery Bay. Tuff is a porous rock formed when volcanic ash gradually hardened after the eruption ceased, over two million years ago.

Vegetation gradually established on Mt Richmond and many hardy native species now grow successfully on the infertile sandy soils occurring in most of the park.

There are no creeks on Mt Richmond. Rain quickly soaks into the sand and seeps down the mountainside and into the deep aquifers. But in places it settles into depressions to form swamps and wet heathlands which are a favourite habitat for birds and other native animals.

Wildflowers About 450 species of plants have been recorded in the park, including 50 orchid species. Correas, heaths, wattles and bush peas provide spectacular colours in spring, but there are plants flowering at Mt Richmond all year around.

The well-drained soils near the summit support a forest dominated by brown stringybark with small pockets of manna gum. Further down the slopes, the main eucalypts are shiny-leaf peppermint and swamp gum (common in the picnic area) with an under-storey of grass trees, heath and many colourful annual and perennial plants. The wet heathlands are dominated by swamp paperbark.

Salt-laden winds have a stunting effect on the vegetation in exposed areas, as you will discover on the Benwerrin Nature Walk.

Wildlife The park's varied habitats support a wide range of wildlife. Eastern grey kangaroos graze near the picnic area, and koalas may be seen in nearby eucalypts in the drier months. Red-necked wallabies occur throughout the park and echidnas can often be seen searching for ants. Look out for copperhead and tiger snakes sunning themselves. Mt Richmond is an important habitat for the uncommon southern potoroo. A small member of the kangaroo family, it is not often seen as it lives in thick undergrowth and is only active at night.

Birds are abundant including the emu, crimson rosella, gang gang cockatoo and Australian raven. Smaller birds include honeyeaters, thornbills, wattlebirds, silver-eyes robins, finches and tree creepers. Among the less common bird species are the southern emu-wren, beautiful firetail, king quail and rufous bristle-bird.

Short walks in the park
The best way to see the park is to take one of the many walks. All the walking tracks are circular, and easy going for people with average levels of fitness.

Benwerrin Nature Walk
Time: 1 hour *Grade:* easy
This nature walk has been designed to introduce you to some of the plants and animals in the park. The walk starts in the picnic area where walking notes are available. Numbered pegs along the track refer to numbers and descriptions in the track notes. If you only have limited time this walk is a must.

Noels Walk
Time: 1 hour *Grade:* easy-medium
The track descends through tall stringybark forest to peppermint and swamp gum open forest at the base of the mount. The last section of the track is fairly steep.

West Walk
Time: 1 hour *Grade:* easy
This walk features good ocean views. Vegetation includes stunted stringybarks and open heathlands. The track may be wet in places during winter and spring.

Ocean View Walk
Time: 45 minutes *Grade:* easy
The walk provides views of Cape Bridgewater and Discovery Bay. Koalas can sometimes be seen feeding on manna gums along the track.

Brushtail Possum

Pink Heath (Epacris impressa), Victoria's State Emblem.

Emu, the world's second largest flightless bird stands over 2 metres tall and runs with a bouncy, swaying motion with speeds up to 45km per hour.

Discovery Bay Coastal Park

A vast stretch of unspoilt ocean beach, huge rolling sand dunes and tranquil lakes and swamps are the dominating features of **Discovery Bay Coastal Park.** This fascinating area occupies the coastal strip between Cape Bridgewater and the Victorian / South Australian border.

Discovery Bay consists of long sandy beaches broken in the north-west half of the bay by rocky promontories jutting out into the surf. Parallel to the beach are extensive mobile dunes, stretching as far as 2.5km inland. The landward fringes of the dunes are bounded by swamps and fresh water lakes, while to the north-west is the Glenelg River estuary.

The park has dramatically changing moods –it can be a very friendly or a very hostile environment. The weather can be quite hot in summer and is subject to strong winds at any time of the year. Unless going for just a short stroll, walkers in the dunes should take care to walk back on their tracks and carry water. It is very easy to get lost.

Bridgewater Lakes

Places to Visit:
Bridgewater Lakes and Caves; Swan Lake, camping and picnic facilities. Lake Mombeong, camping and picnic facilities.

Walks:
Great South West Walk; Swan Lake-short walk through massive sand dunes to coast; and short walks around Lake Mombeong.

Fishing:
Nobles Rocks 12 km south east of Nelson is a favourite surf fishing spot. Surf fishing is also popular in the gutters along the ocean beach with Mulloway, Bream, Shark, and Salmon being caught.

Access into the park is along sealed roads to Bridgewater Lakes, Bridgewater and Nelson beaches or along gravel roads to Swan Lake, Lake Mombeong and Long Swamp from the Portland–Nelson Road. Other minor roads lead into the park from the Portland–Nelson Road.

The Rangers Office at Nelson issues camping permits for tent sites situated at Swan and Monibeong Lakes in the Discovery Bay Coastal Park. Bookings can be made by telephoning or writing to: *Ranger-In-Charge* Lower Glenelg National Park, c/- Post Office, Nelson Vic 3292, Phone : (08) 8738 4051

History of the area:
A number of kitchen middens in the dunes around some of the lakes are the only remaining signs of Aboriginal occupation in the area from a time long before Europeans invaded. The middens are composed of the remains of 1000s of shell-fish meals and occasional flints. The middens range in size from a few square metres to many hectares. There are more than 100 recorded archaeological sites in the park–try not to disturb them. Discovery Bay was divided between two tribes. The western half

was in the territory of the Bunganditj while the eastern half belonged to the Manmeet / Gunditjmara.

Richmond Henty described the Aboriginals around Portland. ...'the natives of the area were a fine looking race, well grown, well fed fellows, reaching beyond average height-for the climate is temperate, the country abounding with game and the rivers teeming with fish'.

On the morning of 3 December 1800, Lieutenant James Grant, in H.M. brig *Lady Nelson* sighted Discovery Bay, becoming the first European recorded to have seen that part of the Australian coast. He described the area as 'flat land covered with brushes and large woods'. However it was Major Mitchell who named Discovery Bay in 1836 after exploring the Glenelg River from Dartmoor to its mouth on Discovery Bay.

Today large bare, moving sand-dunes cover this area. The introduction of stock by European settlers during the 1840s began the stripping of the sensitive coastal vegetation which stabilised the dunes. There is still some private land within the park boundaries and visitors are asked to respect the rights of these property owners.

Swan Lake is probably one of Victoria's most picturesque coastal lakes. Its limpid blue water is hidden between dunes and a small limestone cliff outcrops on the eastern shore. Swimming and picnicking are the main activities at Swan Lake and basic amenities for camping are provided south-east of the picnic area. The lake is suitable for canoeing but motor boats are not allowed.

A walking track follows the course of **Johnstone Creek** through the dunes to the ocean beach, a distance of 1.3km. You can also explore a spectacular waterfall situated on Johnstone Creek upstream of the lake. Water bubbles up from a spring and cascades over a

10 metre drop into the creek.

Access is by gravel road which is sign posted from the main Portland–Nelson Road. The last 3km stretch before reaching Swan Lake is very steep where the road crosses large sand dunes and maybe unsuitable for large caravans.

The Portland Dune Buggy Club has a marked area in the dunes south east of the camping area where they conduct regular race meetings. These machines are something out of 'Thunder Dome' with their roll cages and balloon tyres, that churn up the sand. Within days of their racing the wind has swept away any trace of their tyre tracks and the distant pounding of the surf is the only noise in this unique corner of Victoria.

Lake Mombeong   Access to Lake Mombeong is from the main Portland–Nelson Road, taking Bong Bong Road south through pine plantations before entering the park and continuing a short distance to the lake.

You can camp on the grassy flat on the south eastern shore of Lake Mombeong where fireplaces and a toilet are provided. Canoes, wind surfers, small yachts and small motor boats can be used, but water-skiing is not permitted.

Reflections in Lake Mombeong.

Jackies Lookout is situated in the pine plantation east of Bong Bong Road.

A walking track leads from Lake Mombeong south over dunes which in places reach 20 metres in height before reaching **Sutton's Rocks** on Discovery Bay.

Nobles Rocks   Access is via Quarry Road which leaves the Portland–Nelson Road 800m west of Wade Junction and it is about 6km south to the car-park. The rocks are an excellent place for surf-fishing.

A 3km walk west along the coast from Nobles Rocks, brings you to **Long Swamp** which offers a wide range of opportunities for people interested in flora, fauna and extensive wetlands.

Plant life: The animal and plant communities have altered significantly since Lieutenant Grant sighted the area. Many dunes support no vegetation at all. This is due partly to natural causes, but also to over grazing in the past. The small patches of vegetation that occur on some sand dunes are relic communities indicating that the dunes once supported vegetation. These include plants such as coast wattle, correa, coast beard heath and many others typical of coastal heathlands.

Away from the dune areas, the plant and animal communities are quite complex. At Long Swamp, for example, common reed and bullrushes are replaced in shallower water by sedges and rushes that merge into low heaths and dense paperback thickets. This is a particularly interesting area for botanists because it contains several rare orchids such as the maroon leek orchid the swamp greenhood which occur only in shaded swamp areas.

Around Long Swamp you can also see both pink and yellow flowered forms of a variety of yellow gum (*Eucalyptus leucoxylon* var. *macrocarpa*) that occurs nowhere else in the State.

Animals and birds: On the dunes you will often see the tracks of emus and, if you are lucky, the birds themselves. Along the ocean beaches gulls, dotterels, terns and many other water bird can be found feeding close to the water-line.

Probably the best spot for bird-watching is the estuary at Nelson where spoonbills, pelicans, swans and many other waterbirds are often sighted. The lakes and swamps are also excellent for birds.

Don't go to these areas empty-handed–take a bird book with you. The Gould League books *Birds of Victoria* are particularly useful field guides.

Grey kangaroos and red-necked wallabies are common in the park. At least twelve other native mammals are found in the area, although some are rarely seen. These include pigmy possums, gliders, bush rats and potoroos.

Walking: Although unsafe for swimming and surfing the beaches along Discovery Bay are very good for walking and surf fishing.

Bird watching:
Long Swamp

Pelicans, spoonbills, herons, ducks, freckled ducks, Black Swans, Chestnut Teal are present on the swamp. The coastal scrub habitat supports large numbers of fantails, honeyeaters, flocks of Silvereyes, thornbills, Scrubwrens and Blue-winged Parrots. In the reeds of the swampy areas are Crakes, Little Grass-birds and Reed Wablers.

Wildflowers at Long Swamp, a naturalists paradise.

Massive sand dunes south of Swan Lake.

Lower Glenelg National Park

The Glenelg River has cut a 60 kilometre gorge through limestone in its lower reaches. This gorge is the central feature of the **Lower Glenelg National Park**. Other attractions include the Princess Margaret Rose Cave, the Kentbruck Heath, the Inkpot and Jones Lookout. The park is also on the route of the 250 kilometre 'Great South West Walk', a 10-day walk through forests, river gorges, and coastal dunes commencing and terminating at Portland.

Outdoor education students paddling the Glenelg River Gorge.

History
The first Europeans to explore the Glenelg River were Major Mitchell and his party during their epic journey through Victoria in 1836. In mid August, 16 men led by Mitchell rowed two boats down from Dartmoor to the mouth of the river where they hoped to find a natural harbour. Their hopes were dashed by the shallow and treacherous estuary. Mitchell named the Glenelg after the British Governments Secretary of State for the Colonies. He also named Discovery Bay. The gorge has changed little since it was first seen by Mitchell 150 years ago.

Camping permits can be obtained from the Rangers Office and campsites are for tents only except at Princess Margaret Rose Cave and Pritchards where several sites are available for caravans or campervans.

Plants: The park has a very impressive array of native plants–some 700 species in all. The heath and fringe forest areas are very rich in orchids and the tributaries of Moleside Creek support the most westerly tree fern gullies in Australia.

Wildlife: The eastern grey kangaroo and red-necked wallaby both occur, brush-tailed possums and echidnas are also common. In heath areas many small mammals, including the heath rat, swamp antechinus and potoroo, can be found.

A small colony of wombats located near the Princess Margaret Rose Cave form the only remnants of a once widespread population in south-west Victoria. Similarly, yellow-bellied gliders are now confined to a few bushland areas in the park. The mud lagoon near the river mouth is an important wildlife area.

Birds: Emus, herons and ducks are the most common large birds. Others include the spotted quail thrush, painted quail, ground thrush, azure kingfisher and the rare rufous bristle bird.

PRINCESS MARGARET ROSE CAVES
Of the many limestone caves in the Lower Glenelg National Park, the main cave of the **Princess Margaret Rose Caves** is the most attractive, and is accessible to the public. It contains excellent examples of actively growing stalactites, stalagmites, helictites and other spectacular limestone formations.

How to get there
By Car: The caves are 2km east of the South Australian border and can be reached by a sealed road from Mt. Gambier, or unsealed roads from Nelson, and Dartmoor.
By Boat: The *Nelson Endeavor* a 28 metre passenger launch operates tours to the caves from Nelson. Small boats can also be moored at the caves jetty.

Silver Banksia, Banksia marginata.

Guided tours of the caves are conducted hourly by park rangers on most days.

Picnicking A large picnic area has been developed among the trees near the cave. Wood barbecues, picnic tables and toilets are provided. A small kiosk is open on most days.

Camping Caravan, campervan and tent sites are available at the caves.

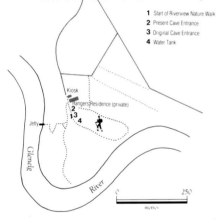

1 Start of Riverview Nature Walk
2 Present Cave Entrance
3 Original Cave Entrance
4 Water Tank

The Discovery of the Caves

Mr S McEachern, Mr J Hutchesson and his son Alan, first explored the cave in 1936 and named it after Princess Margaret. They developed the cave as a tourist attraction with 'Bunny' Hutchesson acting as the first permanent guide, conducting tours from 1941. Since 1980 the cave has been part of Lower Glenelg National Park.

River View Nature Walk

This short walk will show you some of the above ground features of the Princess Margaret Rose Caves system. The walk begins at the cave entrance and follows the line of the caves to vantage points on the Glenelg River.

How to explore the remainder of the park
Driving Gravel and sand roads provide easy access to many parts of the park including the Glenelg River gorge, Jones Lookout, the Inkpot and the Kentbruck Heath.

Scenic Drive

Distance: 80km *Time:* one day
The following drive takes in the most

Princess Margaret Rose Caves

spectacular sections of the gorge and two short walks enable you to take a closer look at the river. The Inkpot and the Kentbruck Heathlands are also included.

From the Park Office take **Bushland Drive** which joins **River Road** just before Sapling Creek picnic area.

The **Sapling Creek Trail** leaves the picnic area and follows the Glenelg River up stream of Wilsons Hall, a camping area on the opposite bank and completes the loop along River Road back to the starting point. The trail is 2.5 km in length and takes one hour at a leisurely walking pace.

Continue driving along River Road to **Forest Camp** and **Battersby's** where there are picnic, camping and boat landing facilities. Stop at **Eaglehawk**

FORMATION OF THE CAVES

Most limestone caves are formed by water seeping down through cracks and faultlines in the limestone, dissolving the rock and creating fissures and tunnels. The formation of Princess Margaret Rose Caves, however, was accelerated by water from the Glenelg River, which worked its way along a faultline for 300m. This occurred 800 000 years ago when the river was 15m above its present height. The water scalloped the walls of the cave and scoured a reasonably level floor.

What to look for
Rainwater, as it seeps from the surface acts as a weak acid to dissolve limestone, producing a solution of calcium bicarbonate. When this reaches the air of the cave, carbon dioxide is released and calcium carbonate is deposited in the form of calcite crystals.

As the solution drips from the cave roof, deposited calcium carbonate is left adhering and a stalactite is formed. Straws are long, thin, hollow stalactites with solution flowing down their centres. Solution dripping from a stalactite builds a stalagmite from the cave floor. If a stalactite and stalagmite join they form a column, and if that thickens it becomes a pillar.

Flow-stone formations are caused by water flowing over the walls, leaving a smooth surface. Other formations visible at the roofline are shawls, blankets and bacons.

Perhaps the most unusual formations in the cave are the mysterious helictites. Defying gravity, these long thin formations grow in different directions. It is not certain how they form, but the commonly accepted theory is that they begin as crystals and are shaped by surface tensions and air currents.

Another mysterious formation in Princess Margaret Rose Caves is the rarely-seen cave coral.

Boating and Water-skiing
Boat-launching ramps are situated at Nelson (one either side of the river), Simsons Landing, Donovans, Sandy Waterholes, Sapling Creek, Wilson Hall, Pritchards and Saunders Landing. Water-skiing and power-boating are permitted at Taylors Straight, which extends upstream from Simsons Landing nearly to the South Australian border and from Sandy Waterholes boat ramp west to Princess Margaret Rose Caves.

Bend where the river turns back on it self providing an excellent vantage point. It is another 3km before you join the Winnap Road and a further 2km to **Pritchards Camp**.

The **Pritchards Nature Trail** hugs the river to **Post & Rail** camp and returns along a section of the 'Great South West Walk' track to Pritchards. The trail is 3.75km in length and takes one hour.

From Pritchards rejoin the Nelson-Winnap Road and turn left towards Dartmoor. Continue north until **Jones Lookout** is sign posted on your left. The Lookout overlooks benched rock faces with the Genelg River below. From Jones Lookout drive south back to the Kentbruck Road intersection and follow this south for a short distance until Inkpot Road. The **Inkpot** is about 2km east along this track. Picnic tables and wood barbecues are located near the Inkpot. The distinctive inky black water in the pool is caused by the decomposition of organic material from the surrounding vegetation.

Retrace your route back to the Kentbruck Road and turn south until Skyline Road is sign posted on your left. Skyline Road borders the **Kentbruck Heath** country where wildflowers are a blaze of colour during Spring. Stop anywhere along this track and wander through the heathland. Skyline Road continues south until it intersects the

CANOEING

The majestic **Glenelg River** is one of Victoria's grandest waterways. The river rises in the Grampians and winds 400km across western Victoria to the sea. The best way to experience the **Glenelg River Gorge** is by canoe or boat. The river is wide, rarely less than 50 metres, and very deep. It is navigable for more than 70km upstream of Nelson.

As the Glenelg enters the national park it passes over a series of rapids cut into limestone which mark the beginning of the spectacular gorge which extends to the rivers mouth at Nelson. The limestone was formed 25-40 million years ago on the floor of a shallow sea. The sea level dropped and the Glenelg River gradually carved the spectacular gorge.

In places the cliffs are sheer, sometimes they are gently sloped and covered in scrub. The forests and flag reeds which flank the river abound in wildlife.

The National Parks Service has constructed eleven canoe camps between **Dartmoor** and **Simsons Landing** which make it possible to paddle the entire gorge and spend the nights in small bush camps with landing jetties, fresh water, toilets and fire places. The canoe camps greatest appeal is that the majority of them are only accessible by water.

There are several options when planning a canoeing trip on the Glenelg River. Paddling upstream from Simsons Landing; putting in at Dartmoor and canoeing downstream to Nelson, or

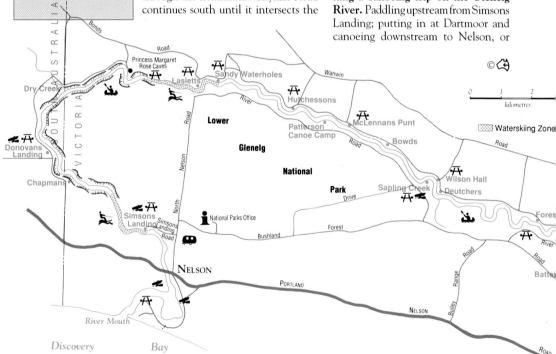

main Portland-Nelson Road. Turn west for the 20km run back to Nelson.

Walking   Many fire-access tracks run through the park providing a range of walks. Short walks commence at Sapling Creek, Pritchards and at the Princess Margaret Rose Caves.

paddling small sections of the gorge between points where there is road access. Distances between each canoe camp are marked on the map down stream from Dartmoor. The total distance between Dartmoor and Simsons Landing at Nelson is 71km.

For the safety and the convenience of

river users, the Glenelg River has been zoned for various uses. There are two water-skiing/power-boating zones at Taylors Straight and Sandy Waterholes. Transit channels marked with signs and buoys have been defined to provide passage for slower boats and canoes through water-skiing/power-boating zones.

There are a number of boat-launching ramps along the river and these are shown on the map together with the principal landings. Vehicle access to canoe camps is only available at Moleside and Pritchards.

Hiking the 'Great South West Walk'.

Glenelg River

THE GREAT SOUTH WEST WALK

The 250km walk provides an excellent introduction to the fascinating variety of scenery and wildlife in south west Victoria. The walk is not solely for hardened bushwalkers. It can be undertaken in easy stages by young and old alike. The walk has 16 campsites ranging from 9-22km apart which provide fresh water, toilets and fire places. There are stiles, steps and bridges installed over rivers and streams so that the walk can be tackled anytime of the year. The track starts and finishes at the Portland Visitor Information Centre and is signposted with the distinctive red arrow reassurance markers .

THE FIRST SECTION
Portland - Nine Mile Flora and Fauna Reserve to Moleside.
Distance: 62km.
After a 12km walk north of Portland the track goes through open forest and crosses the Surrey and Fitzroy Rivers.

THE SECOND SECTION
Moleside to Nelson
Distance: 45km
Nearing the end of the forest the walk meets the Glenelg River at Moleside and follows its winding path to it's mouth at Nelson.

THE THIRD SECTION
Nelson Beach to Descartes Bay
Distance: 55km.
Leaving the Glenelg River mouth near Nelson, the walk turns east along the seemingly endless beaches and rolling sand dunes of Discovery Bay.

As a diversion from the white sands , detour to the fresh water lakes Monibeong and Swan or visit Mt Richmond National Park and climb the lookout to search out your journeys end.

THE FINAL LEG
Descartes Bay to Portland
Distance: 48km
As the walk heads back to Portland it winds its way along the rugged clifftops of Discovery, Bridgewater and Nelson Bays.Finally the walk winds its way back to Portland through coastal heathland with harbour views.

Canoes are available for hire in Nelson and transport can be arranged to Dartmoor to commence your trip. The *Nelson Endeavour* operates tours of the gorge, including visits to Princess Margaret Rose Caves.

When using the river, canoes and boats must not be beached or moored amongst the reeds, or obstruct boat-launching ramps. *Canoeists require a permit from the Rangers Office for camping overnight at canoe-camps.*

Canoeists are asked to take their rubbish with them when they leave the park.

VOLCANOES
& SINKHOLES

NELSON TO MT GAMBIER

Nelson to Mt Gambier

59 kilometres (via Port MacDonnell) or *36 kilometres (via Princes Highway)*

AT A GLANCE
NELSON
River cruises, boat and
canoe hire, excellent
estuary fishing.
Distance:
544 km from Melbourne
565 km via Cape
Bridgewater

Tourist Information:
*Nelson Information
Centre*
Phone: (08) 8738 4220

*Lower Glenelg National
Park, Nelson*
Phone: (08) 8738 4051

Accommodation:
1 Motel
2 Guset Houses
1 Hotel
1 Caravan Park
1 Bed & Breakfast

Picnic Spots:
Estuary Beach

The undulating plains dominated by the extinct volcanic craters of
Mt Schank and Mt Gambier give no clue to the beauty below the
surface in limestone sinkholes. The formation of the south east corner of
South Australia has been influenced by two major factors-volcanic
activity and changing sea levels. The area has been submerged many
times over the last forty million years and the accumulation of dead
marine organisms have formed massive beds of limestone which now
underlays the region. As rainwater percolates down joints and fissures
the limestone is dissolved, to form tunnels and networks of caves.

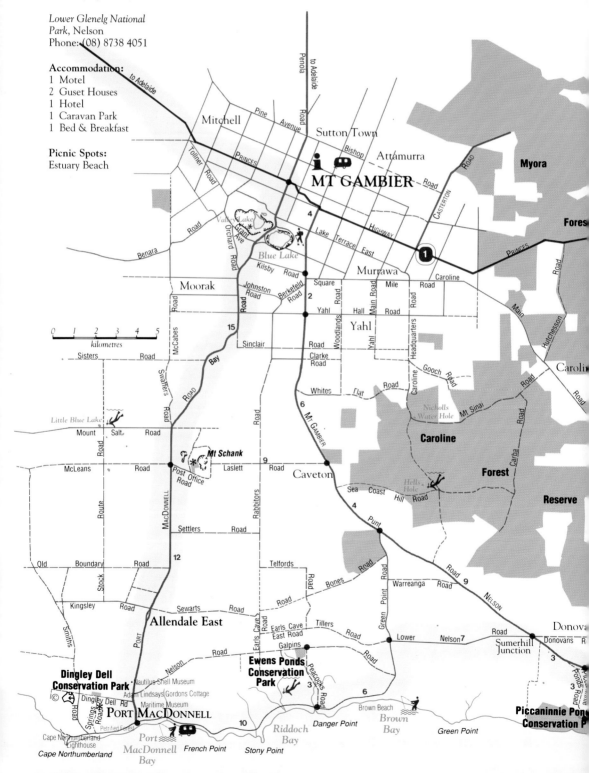

120

Volcanic eruptions occured as recently as 5000 years ago and are remembered in the legends of local Aboriginal tribes. The vibrant blue coloured crater lakes at Mt Gambier are now a source of great curiosity as they regularly change colour.

You do not have to be a skin diver to explore the hidden world at Piccaninnie and Ewens Ponds. All that is needed is a snorkel and a pair of flippers to help you peer through crystal clear water into deep fissures and submerged caverns lined with exotic aquatic plants.

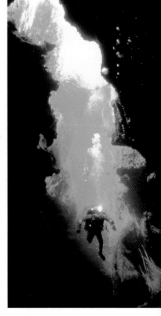

Scuba diving in the crystal clear waters of Piccaninnie Ponds

PREVIOUS PAGES
Blue Lake, Mt Gambier

Nelson is a small township straddling the Portland/Mt Gambier Road at the mouth of the Glenelg River. Surrounded by the Lower Glenelg National Park this is a wonderful place to stay and discover the flora and fauna of the park. Motels, guesthouses, hotel and caravan accommodation as well as boat and canoe hire facilities are available.

Nelson is also one of Victoria's best estuary fishing destinations.

The high level bridge at Nelson is 4km from the South Australian State Border where there is a time gain of half an hour. Another 2km west is a signposted gravel road running 2km south into Piccaninnie Ponds Conservation Park.

Piccaninnie Ponds Conservation Park Much of Piccanininnie Pond's beauty lies beneath the surface. Crystal clear water fills massive caverns. These can be explored by properly equipped and experienced divers. A jetty has been constructed close to the main car-park for divers entering and leaving the ponds so there is minimum disturbance to the bottom or plant life. The jetty is also an excellent place for non-divers to look down into the amazing clear waters of the ponds. Visibility underwater can exceed 40 metres.

The Piccaninnie Ponds were formed with the dissolving of limestone along a fault line forming the network of caverns and tunnels. The ponds are bounded by a stable coastal sand-dune to the south and low calcerite dunes to the north. Prior to 1906 water from the main ponds wetlands flowed east, fed the eastern swamp and discharged into the Glenelg River. However it now flows south to the coast via the Picaninnie Ponds Outlet via a channel dug through dunes to the sea between 1917 and 1945.

Before diving or snorkelling you must have a current permit issued by the South Australian *Department of Environment and Natural Resources* who manage the Piccaninnie Ponds Conservation Park.

The Glenelg River at Nelson

River Cruises & Canoe Hire:

The *Nelson Endeavour* and *Glenelg River Cruises* operate cruises upstream to the Princess Margaret Rose Caves. The cruises depart from the main landing at Nelson on Wednesdays and Saturdays at 1pm Victorian time. Additional tours operate over December and January school holidays. There are no cruises during July and August. Phone: (08) 8738 4191 or (08) 8738 4192.

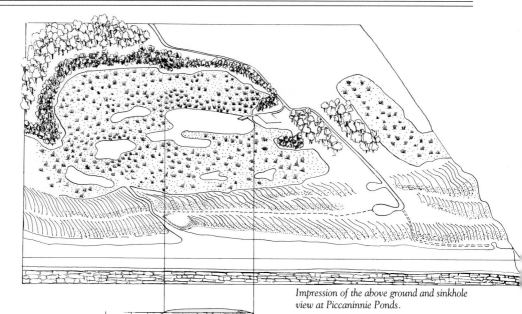

Impression of the above ground and sinkhole view at Piccaninnie Ponds.

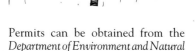

FORMATION OF A SINKHOLE

Rainwater soaks into the limestone

The carbon dioxide in the rainwater dissolves the limestone along lines of weakness

The dissolving action increases the size of the cracks, until blocks of limestone collapse from the ceiling

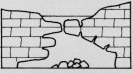

The ceiling may collapse forming a sinkhole

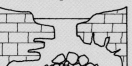

The process continues, and can extend to depths of over 80 metres.

Permits can be obtained from the *Department of Environment and Natural Resources* at 11 Helen street, Mt Gambier or by phoning (08) 8735 1177.

Diving in the ponds can be dangerous due to the cold waters, (15-16°C), disturbance of fine silt causing blackouts, and deep diving causing nitrogen narcosis (which impairs reasoning, memory and judgement).

Diving in clear water

Other attractions in the Park

Two walking tracks leave the lower carpark. One runs west between the coastal dunes giving access to the Ponds Outlet Channel and interesting limestone formations on the beach. The other track heads south over the dunes and east along the beach to fresh water springs bubbling out of the sand at low tide about an hours walk from the coastal car-park.

During spring the coastal heath near the northern boundary of the park is alive with colour.

Camping is allowed near the beach in the shelter of coastal wattle.

Summer Hill Junction is the next intersection after passing the State Border. Donovans Landing, a holiday village on the banks of the Glenelg River is 4km east along a gravel road, and Port MacDonnell is 23km west.

From Summer Hill Junction there are two alternative routes to Mt Gambier. The most direct route takes you 27km into Mt Gambier past pine plantations and views of Mt Schank, an extinct volcano.

The jetty at Piccaninnie Ponds

Route via Port MacDonnell

The **more scenic alternative route via Port MacDonnell** is 50km, but a magnificent drive through rich dairying country with extensive views of the dunes along Discovery Bay to the east and Riddoch Bay to the west is rewarding. Highlights include Ewens Ponds, Brown Bay surf beach, Port MacDonnell rock-lobster fishing fleet, Cape Northumberland lighthouse, Adam Lindsay Gordon's Cottage, Mt Schank and Little Blue Lake.

Ewens Ponds is another wonderland of underwater chambers and caves. The reserve is managed by the South Australian Department of Lands in Mt Gambier. Snorkelling is permitted without a permit, however an efficient thick (5mm) full length wetsuit must be worn.

Scuba Divers must adhere to regulations and complete the forms available on site before diving in the ponds.

If snorkelling, start your swim from the landing near the car-park at Pond 1 and leave the water at the landing in Pond 3. The current will effortlessly carry you along the creek through the ponds. A walking track links the two landings.

An extended snorkel dive is possible by continuing through Ewens Ponds along Eight Mile Creek to the coast. The total swim is about 2.4km but is assisted by the stream flow. It is recommended that you arrange to be picked up at the end of the swim.

The Department of Environment and Natural Resources has produced guidelines for scuba and snorkel diving in Ewens Ponds to avoid damage to the aquatic environment to maintain the amazing water clarity for all divers.
You must:
- enter and exit from the water only at landings erected in ponds one and three or in Eight Mile Creek down stream of the ponds.
- swim well above the bottom so as not to disturb the silt or vegetation.
- plants should not be touched or disturbed by your wash as the surface of each large plant supports its own delicate algae and animal community.
- no camping, boating or fishing.
- vehicles are restricted to designated car-parks.

There are other sinkholes in the area which are well worth a visit. The main road between Port MacDonnell and Mt Gambier divides around a sinkhole at **Allendale East Township** which was used to water bullock teams. It also attracts skin divers.

Brown Bay Spectacular surf beach.

Cape Northumberland

PORT MACDONNELL

Port MacDonnell is home to the largest rock-lobster fishing fleet in South Australia. Between October and April the fleet can be seen leaving the port to fish the depths of the Southern Ocean. The catch either ends up a delicacy in a local restaurant or airfreighted live overseas.

Built in the 1860s the **Old Customs House** is a fine example of colonial architecture and gives an indication of how busy the port was when early settlers were sending their produce to Adelaide and Melbourne.

The **Woolwash & Harbour View caravan park** is right on the foreshore at Port MacDonnell and fronts an excellent swimming beach. Explore the network of walking tracks along the dunes and cliffs at Port MacDonnell.

AT A GLANCE
PORT MACDONNELL
Rock-lobster fishing port
Distance:
567 km from Melbourne
597 km via Cape Bridgewater

Accommodation:
1 Motel
2 Caravan Parks

Picnic spots:
Clarke Park off Springs Road. Picnic tables and barbecues are placed among the contorted coastal gums.

Attractions:
Cape Northumberland lighthouse, Adam Lindsay Gordon's Cottage, Maritime Museum.

Old Customs House

The locals claim the lobsters from Port MacDonnell are the best.

Port MacDonnell Maritime Museum, 47 Meylin Street gives an insight into the South Easts maritime history. *Open:* Sunday, Wednesday and Public Holidays,10am–2pm. Admission is charged.

Nautilus Shell Museum, 2km from Port MacDonnell on Bay Road, has an international shell collection. *Open:* Sundays and school and public holidays.

Cape Northumberland

The original'MacDonnell Light' on Cape Northumberland first lit up the rugged coastline in January 1859. It was a 8.5m high lighthouse erected on a rocky headland 30m above the surf. It was built in such an exposed position that the keepers reported the very foundations shuddered during heavy storms. A new lighthouse was built on higher ground in 1882.

A memorial is the only trace of the original 'MacDonnell Light'. It commemorates the first keeper, Captain Ben Germein who played a heroic role in the rescue of survivors from the shipwreck of the *S.S.Admella* in 1859. The new lighthouse flashes a warning beam 40 km out to sea. The earlier light had been difficult to see during storms. It is not possible to inspect the lighhouse since its conversion to automatic operation in 1979.

Adam Lindsay Gordon's Cottage, Dingley Dell Conservation Park. There are guided tours at the historic home of Adam Lindsay Gordon, horseman and poet 1835-70. The cottage is open Sundays and school holidays 10am to 4pm and weekdays by appointment. Phone: (08) 8738 2221 Admission is charged.

Adam Lindsay Gordon's cottage

Adam Lindsay Gordon's Obelisk off John Watson Drive, Mt Gambier was erected as a memorial to the poet and acknowledges his daring horsemanship. From near this spot in 1864 Gordon made his famous leap over the old post and rail guard fence onto the narrow ledge overlooking the lake.

Gordon's Leap Cliff top hurdle is the location of one of the most daring exploits of Australian horsemanship. Adam Lindsay Gordon was out riding with a party of friends playing follow the leader, and known for his daring and recklessness he challenged the others to follow him. Urging his horse to full gallop, he raced forward towards a high post-and-rail fence and beyond it a 2 metre wide ledge. The ledge was the rim of Blue Lake and a 110m drop to the rocks and water below. While his friends looked on in horror, he cleared the fence, turned the horse in mid-air and landed safely, only centimetres from death.

Allendale East The road divides around a sinkhole. Ye Olde Post Office Tea Rooms serve home made pastries and Devonshire teas most days.

Mount Schank This is an extinct volcano,158 m high, half way between Port Macdonnell and Mount Gambier. It has a walking track to the crater rim where the views of the surrounding districts are breathtaking. The track continues down into the crater with its sheets of exposed lava.

The main crater has always been dry but a small crater on the southern slopes of Mount Schank once held three metres of water, teamed with fish and contained a floating island. It dried up in the 1940s drought and all trace of the floating island has disappeared.

Barbecues and picnic facilities are provided in the car-park.

The cone shape of Mt Schank crater is clearly visible.

Little Blue Lake is 3kms west of Mt Schank. This lake is similar to the Blue Lake in Mt Gambier, and it changes colour to a vivid blue in mid November.

Little Blue Lake

Mt Gambier

A garden city encircles the mysterious crater lake that changes from a dark grey to a deep cobalt blue during the summer months. Blue Lake at Mt Gambier is one of Australia's best known tourist attractions and it's unspoiled beauty attracts thousands of visitors.

Mt Gambier is the western gateway to Australia's Southern Touring Route which hugs the coastline for 550 kilometres to emerge at Geelong in Victoria.

Lady Nelson Visitor and Discovery Centre is located at the corner of Jubilee Highway and Penola Road, in Lady Nelson Park.

This is a most imaginative centre giving visitors an insight into the natural and man made history of Mount Gambier and the south east region of South Australia.

Once inside the centre Lieutenant Grant in the replica of his brig the *Lady Nelson* tells his story of discovery. You then step back into geological time when erupting volcanos dominated the landscape. Continue over the floor of a fossil cave and watch an excellent film on diving in local sinkholes.

Blue Lake, Mt Gambier

Lieutenant Grant and the Lady Nelson.

Finally the visitor is led through a sand dune environment with an Aboriginal midden and along an elevated walkway which takes you through the wetland, an important feature of this part of Australia.

A series of Heritage, Lake Walks and Drives with historic notes on the city's finest old buildings have been produced

by the local Mt Gambier Heritage Society. Don't forget to pick up these excellent brochures when visiting the centre.

The Heritage Walks Include:
City Centre The historic buildings of the city are featured on this walk.

Church Hill This includes two of Mt Gambier's earliest churches, overlooking the entrance to the city.

Templar Terrace Includes the old Court House and Lake Terrace.

Vansittart Park These peaceful gardens were established 100 years ago.

Heritage Drives-North and South Drive Some of the early architecture and buildings constructed in Mt Gambier Stone, the distinctive white building stone unique to Mt Gambier, are located along the routes.

Lakes Walks
Blue Lake Grand Circuit This is an easy 5km walk on a paved track around the rim of the Blue Lake Crater. It takes less than one hour.

Leg of Mutton Lake An easy 1.6km walk starting at Rook Walk Lookout, a small pavilion, and dropping down into the Leg of Mutton Crater. It takes approximately 45 minutes.

Mountain Trail a 4.2km trail leaves Marks Lookout and climbs the rim of Valley Lake crater to Centenary Tower.

AT A GLANCE
MOUNT GAMBIER
Distance:
603 km from Melbourne
624 Km via Cape Bridgewater

Tourist Information:
Lady Nelson Visitor and Discovery Centre,
Cnr. Jubilee Highway and Penola Road,
Mount Gambier 5290
Phone: (08) 8724 1730
Toll Free 1800 087 187

Accommodation:
20 Motels
3 Hotels
6 Caravan Parks
Several Bed & Breakfast

Attractions:
Crater Lakes, beautiful gardens, caves and home of South Australia's soft wood industry

Picnic Spots:
Lakes Recreation Area
Vansittart Park

Vansittart Park gardens

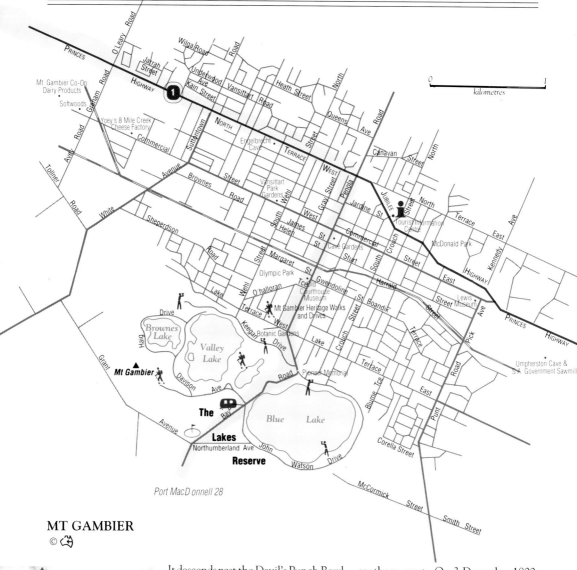

Port MacDonnell 28

MT GAMBIER
© 🦘

Town Hall, Mt Gambier

It descends past the Devil's Punch Bowl to Davison Drive and Marks Lookout. This is the most strenuous walk, however the views from Centenary Tower are well worth the effort. Allow 2-3 hours to complete the walk.

Pepperpot Trail This 1.7km walk also starts at Mark's Lookout and circles the Leg of Mutton Crater. It is an easy walk that can be covered in one hour.

***Three Short Walks*-Brownes Lake** is an easy 1.2km walk which takes about 45 minutes. It passes the Henty Monument and a wildlife reserve; **Blue Gum** is a 2.3km circular walk which starts in the Centenary Tower car-park. The path passes through a stand of blue gums, with views to Mt Schank. It takes about 35 minutes at an easy pace.

The Oaks off Shepherdson Road near Tenison College is a beautiful walk through an oak grove. The circular route is 1.4km and takes about 40 minutes at an easy pace.

Brief history of the City
Mt Gambier was named by Lieutenant James Grant while navigating the southern coast. On 3 December 1800 he sighted two peaks from his ship and named the most prominent after Lord Gambier and the closer one after Admiral Schanck, the designer of the centre board keel used in his ship, the *Lady Nelson*.

It was not until 1839 that Stephen Henty and party seeking new grazing land beyond their settlement at Portland climbed Mt Gambier and saw the beauty of the lakes. By 1841 they built a hut on the land between the Valley and Brownes Lake and set their herds grazing the area. Henty's hut is commemorated by a cairn built from basalt quarried from Mt Schank. Rough cut limestone blocks from the chimney of the hut are incorporated into the base of the memorial.

Another hut was built on the west side of a cave (now the Cave Gardens in the City Centre) where there was a plentiful fresh water supply. Henty lost the rights to the land to Evelyn Sturt, younger brother of the explorer Captain James Sturt, when he secured a lease from the South Australian Government. Henty was under the impression he was still within the boundaries of New South Wales at the time.

Mt Gambier was first surveyed in 1854. In 1856 a Public House and Barracks were erected from stone quarried from the west of town.

In 1876 the first pinus radiata trees were planted in the district and by 1920 the South Australian Woods and Forests department had established large forests. Mills were opened at Mount Burr, Nangwarry and Mt Gambier and timber is now a major industry to the city.

Mt Gambier was constituted a municipality in 1876, the rail link was connected to Adelaide in 1879 and it proclaimed a city in 1955.

Major Attractions

Blue Lake turns cobalt blue in late November and remains that way until late March each year, when it reverts to winter grey. Scientists from Flinders University and the CSIRO have come up with a theory that the groundwater entering the crater is supersaturated with calcium bicarbonate and the calcite crystals precipitate out at a faster rate during summer when the water is warmer.

Blue Lake Pumping Station is open for tours daily except on Christmas Day.

Valley, Browns and Leg of Mutton Lakes These are west of the Blue Lake City Caravan Park, turn right at the round about, adjacent to Blue Lake. Picnic facilities and barbecues are provided. There is also a boardwalk, wildlife reserve and childrens play ground.

Umpherston Sinkhole, Engelbrecht Cave, Jubilee Highway West
Open daily with tours on the hour 12noon–3pm conducted by 'Life Line South East'. See the cave and water level at the viewing platform. Admission is charged.

Old Court House Museum, Bay Road. The court house opened in 1865 and was in continuous use until the new court house was built. The Museum still contains the original fixtures and furnishings. Experience standing in a cell or sitting in the judges chair. Open: 12noon to 4pm, Sunday to Friday.

C.S.R. Softwoods. The operation at Mt Gambier is the company's largest mill, covering 36 hectares. Here you can see the latest in timber handling equipment and technology. Guided tours can br arranged through the Lady Nelson and Discovery Visitor Centre.

Carter Holt Harvey Timber Tours. Jubilee Highway East. This mill opened in 1958 and is the largest of its kind in the Southern Hemisphere. The main timber species milled is pinus radiata. Guided tours can be arranged through the Lady Nelson Visitor and Discovery Centre.

Umpherston Cave

FORMATION OF A CRATER LAKE

Initial explosive eruption. Hot magma encounters water in the limestone, causing huge cloud of steam.

Explosive eruption. Vent deepens. Crater walls build and debris rain over surrounding country side.

Formation of cone. Lava fountaining produces small scoria cones.

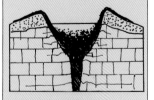

Formation of the crater lake results when the volcanic activity ceases, and unstable deposits of the cone slump inwards.

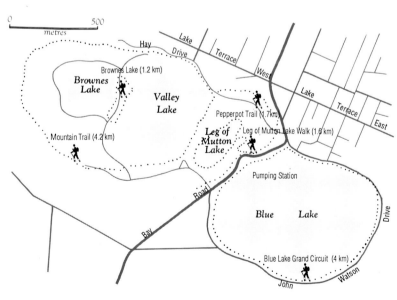

WALKS AROUND THE LAKES

© ⚑

INDEX